COLLECTED PLAYS OF
FRANCIS QUINLAN

COLLECTED PLAYS OF FRANCIS QUINLAN

VOLUME ONE

ISBN: 069241746X
ISBN 13: 9780692417461

Library of Congress Control Number: 2015905151
BardArts, Staten Island, New York

Contact: bardarts@verizon.net

CONTENTS

HENRIETTA

Time and Place

Julian Crosse's Office, the *Gazette*, a daily newspaper
New York City, Mid-June, 1922

Characters

Freddy, Third Assistant Office Manager
Henrietta Zachariah, a lady with a complaint and a pistol
Julian Crosse, Chief Editor
Emil Harthauser, Publisher
Krystal Kracker, Assistant to the Publisher
Lovie, a Gangster
James McGurk, NYPD Detective
Margaret Sanger, Feminist
Lou, NYPD Detective (non-speaking)
Katrina Crowley, Job Applicant
Jarret Thorne, Job Applicant
Henry Hardstone, Job Applicant

Casting note: The show can be performed by four men and two women. The roles of Crosse and Thorne are performed by the same actor. This also applies to the Krystal/Katrina and Harthauser/Hardstone roles. The actor playing McGurk can easily double as Lovie. Any of the actors can play Lou (non-speaking, brief appearance). The actress who plays Krystal can double as Margaret Sanger, who appears in one scene.

ACT ONE

June, 1922, when New Yorkers got their information from newspapers (no TV or internet). Julian Crosse's office at the *Gazette*. FREDDY enters and sets inter-office mail in the in-box. HENRIETTA slips in behind him. A handsome woman in her mid-thirties, she wears a tailored jacket, skirt and a custom blouse. FREDDY turns about and sees her.

FREDDY: Oh! You should not be here! There is a waiting room—

HENRIETTA: Excuse me, but I can't talk to someone without knowing his name.

FREDDY: My name is Freddy, but that's not the point—

HENRIETTA: Nice to meet you, Freddy. I am Henrietta. I am here to see Mr. Crosse.

FREDDY: Mr. Crosse is at lunch. Do you have an appointment?

HENRIETTA: No, but Mr. Crosse has reason to talk to me. [Sits] This looks like a comfortable chair.

FREDDY: I was about to explain that this will cost me my job. When Mr. Crosse leaves orders that no one is to enter this room, he is very serious.

HENRIETTA: You won't lose your job. I will explain the circumstances to Mr. Crosse.

FREDDY: He won't listen to explanations. He has a very short fuse—especially with masculine employees.

HENRIETTA: Suppose you were a woman. What would he do?

FREDDY: It depends. Am I beautiful or a plain Jane?

HENRIETTA: You are a beauty—a blonde, a ripe peach.

FREDDY: Say no more. Mr. Crosse would come on like a horny dog.

HENRIETTA: And—?

FREDDY: The blonde might take him on. Me? I'd be fired.

HENRIETTA: What is your job, Freddy?

FREDDY: Third assistant office manager. I get the junk jobs—the ones no one else wants.

HENRIETTA: Mr. Crosse won't fire you. I won't allow it. I own fifty-one percent of this newspaper's stock.

FREDDY: Wow! Let me get you a cup of coffee.

HENRIETTA: Is it fresh?

FREDDY: Brewed three minutes ago.

HENRIETTA: Milk, not too light, one sugar cube.

FREDDY dashes off. HENRIETTA removes a pistol from her purse, aims it at Crosse's chair, and returns it to her purse. A few moments pass. JULIAN CROSSE enters. In his mid-forties, he is handsome in a rumpled, world-weary way.

CROSSE: Are you comfortable?

HENRIETTA: Quite.

CROSSE: Where is Freddy?

HENRIETTA: Awfully nice young man.

CROSSE: Keeping my office secured is his top job. He failed to do it. That will cost him his job.

HENRIETTA: Would you really fire him for something as trivial as that?

CROSSE: Information kept in this office is for my eyes only. Visitors are welcome only if I am here to receive them.

HENRIETTA: I hope you will make an exception in this case. Freddy was delivering your mail. I came in behind him. He pleaded with me to leave. The poor boy was ready to cry—until I gave him reason not to worry.

CROSSE: Indeed! What is the reason?

HENRIETTA: We will come to that later. First I would like to reason with you.

> **FREDDY enters with a cup of coffee. Hands it to HENRIETTA.**

FREDDY: I am sorry, Mr. Crosse. She sneaked in while I was delivering your mail. Wouldn't budge.

CROSSE: I know, Freddy. We will discuss it later.

FREDDY: Her name is Henrietta. Did she tell you—

HENRIETTA: I will do my own telling, Freddy.

FREDDY: Yes ma'am. [**To CROSSE**] Would you like a cup of coffee?

CROSSE: No. Leave.

HENRIETTA: Thanks for the coffee, Freddy.

FREDDY: You're welcome.

FREDDY closes the door as he exits.

CROSSE: Henrietta ... Have we met?

HENRIETTA: Yes, but I didn't come to talk about that. My full name is Henrietta Zachariah.

CROSSE: I take it that you are Mrs. Roderick Zachariah.

HENRIETTA: I am.

CROSSE: Does your husband know you are here?

HENRIETTA: No. I am acting on my own. I am very upset at the attitude you are taking toward Roderick. He is a good husband and father. You are persecuting a good man.

CROSSE: Persecuting! Your husband is not a saint. He is a well paid public servant. He is in charge of the city's finances. Irregularities have been uncovered; some payments look like payoffs. It is a newspaper's duty to investigate and report.

HENRIETTA: At a meeting in the mayor's office— with all sorts of prominent people present—Roderick corrected several errors in statements made by your publisher, Mr. Harthauser. Two months later he finds himself the object of a journalistic investigation. Clearly there is a vendetta.

CROSSE: Statements made by Mr. Harthauser and the editorial staff are frequently challenged; we take it in stride. It does not influence the way we do our job. You, on the other hand, cannot be objective. You love your husband: love blinds you to his failings.

HENRIETTA: I am a very clear-sighted person—even where love is involved.

CROSSE: Clear-sighted. I'll bet you are. ... I have met you, though I can't recall the occasion.

HENRIETTA: Two years ago. Gabriella Vanderhoff's reception for some French diplomats.

CROSSE: That's it! I am delighted that you remember me.

HENRIETTA: How could I forget? You came on like a—well, ah—

CROSSE: Like what? Come on, out with it.

HENRIETTA: A horny dog.

CROSSE: [Laughs] I see that you have been talking to Freddy. If I was a little overbearing at Gabriella's party, I apologize. But then, you didn't run.

HENRIETTA: I couldn't run: you had me backed up against a wall. I was a wallflower. After the reception, my friends teased me about it.

CROSSE: I remember your eyes, apprehensive, yet intrigued ...

HENRIETTA: I did not come to discuss your sex appeal.

CROSSE: Of course not. You are here to plead for your husband.

HENRIETTA: Those headlines are destroying him. They are ruining my life and my children's lives. At school, the children have endured endless taunts. A chorus chanting, "your daddy is a crook," is not easy for children to take. They are now housebound. I had to hire a tutor to teach them. Every person of any reputation snubs me. My social life is non-existent.

CROSSE: This would be avoided if your husband conducted his professional affairs with greater discretion.

Your unhappiness is his fault, not ours. We are simply doing our job.

HENRIETTA: You are inventing a scandal. You have nothing concrete, in spite of the fact that you are bribing a member of Roderick's staff to leak documents to you.

CROSSE: We are bribing no one. Be careful what you say: if you name someone and it becomes public knowledge, you could be open to a lawsuit.

HENRIETTA: Very well, I withdraw the word bribe, but I will name the woman: Genevieve Martin. She is employed in Roderick's office. You and she have been seen together three times at that Tibetan restaurant. What is it called?

CROSSE: Benares.

HENRIETTA: Benares is a city in India.

CROSSE: It is Buddhism's holiest city—otherwise known as Varanasi.

HENRIETTA: Are you a Buddhist?

CROSSE: Spiritually, yes.

HENRIETTA: On one occasion, Genevieve Martin passed papers to you.

CROSSE: I take it that you hired a detective.

HENRIETTA: I disliked doing it, but—

CROSSE: —it was necessary.

HENRIETTA: Unfortunately.

CROSSE: Genevieve and I are friends. That is all there is to it. The papers she gave me had nothing to do with your husband's affairs. I swear it.

HENRIETTA: Does Genevieve's husband know of your friendship?

CROSSE: You are being amateurish. The scandal you have uncovered is small-change.

CROSSE cannot suppress a yawn.

HENRIETTA: Do I bore you?

CROSSE: You don't bore me, I bore myself. I am world-weary, indifferent to all fates, including my own. When I was a young reporter, I spent two years in Tibet doing a series of stories for a magazine. They wanted me to plumb the depths of Tibetan society, find out if there is anything to the spiritual life they live, a life in which every individual seeks to discover karma—his personal Truth. It was a fascinating assignment. I discovered Buddhism. ... **[Abrupt]** Does your husband love you?

HENRIETTA: That question is like a slap in the face!

CROSSE: He has had mistresses—three in the last five years. I can prove it.

HENRIETTA: **[Shocked]** I hope you are not going to publish that story. It would hurt me even more than Roderick.

CROSSE: If it becomes necessary, I will publish it.

HENRIETTA: Have you no conscience?

CROSSE: I am a journalist. I must put truth ahead of conscience.

HENRIETTA: I hoped you would be decent. You are not. You force me to bring my story to another newspaper.

CROSSE: The newspaper business in this city is savagely competitive. We compete for stories, but we do not attack each other.

HENRIETTA: The fact that you are dating a member of Roderick's staff ought to be of interest to at least one editor.

CROSSE: Not one of my fellow editors is an innocent. I can retaliate. They know it.

HENRIETTA: [**Paces**] You are cruel and I am helpless—as only a woman can be helpless. To be utterly defeated—crushed by a man's arrogance—I hate it! ... No, no, no—NO! I will not give up! I will fight back!

> **HENRIETTA removes the pistol from her purse, aims it at CROSSE.**

HENRIETTA: When I shoot you, every paper will publish my story.

CROSSE: You can't be serious!

HENRIETTA: I have never in my life been more serious.

CROSSE: [**Speaks quickly, urgently**] If you use that weapon, you and your family will be ruined. Your husband will be forced to resign. You will be dragged through a nasty, very public trial. Your children will live in disgrace, their mother, an assassin, a jailbird.

> **CROSSE rises from his chair. He talks as he approaches her, one cautious step at a time. HENRIETTA retreats until she is up against a wall.**

CROSSE: Imagine spending the rest of your days in prison. A grey world, a drab existence. Awful food. No fine clothes, no fashionable society, no fancy balls—a life without the joy of raising your children. When your husband gets out of jail—figure three years with an early release—he will remarry and declare that he has at last found the right woman. Your children will by degrees erase you from their memories. It is an old story. People in the newspaper business know it all too well. ... I am extending a hand to you, a compassionate hand, the hand of a man who once looked into your eyes and saw a beautiful soul, who sees the same soul now—

One more step. HENRIETTA, who is almost under CROSSE's spell, hesitates, starts to lower the pistol, then quickly raises it again.

CROSSE: —the man you must obey. ... Now, place the pistol in my hand ...

BANG! A shot is heard. It sounds more like a firecracker than a gunshot. CROSSE steps back. He rubs his shoulder where he was hit.

CROSSE: Ouch! ... A little blood, no real pain, only a sting. Do you call that a gun? It is more like a pea shooter. I feel nothing more than a sting—a bee sting. [An awesome realization] A bee sting! That which was foretold has happened! ... I feel dizzy. ... I must sit.

CROSSE staggers toward his desk and flops into the seat.

CROSSE: That was not a nice thing to do!

HENRIETTA: You almost had me talked out of it, Mr. Crosse—until you played Svengali, attempting to impose your sexual superiority on me.

CROSSE: You said you were a wallflower. I believed you. You lied.

CROSSE lowers his head on to the desk. A knock at the door, FREDDY's voice is heard. HENRIETTA restores the pistol to her purse.

FREDDY: Mr. Crosse! Is everything all right? [Enters.] I heard a noise. It sounded like a firecracker. [Addresses HENRIETTA] What happened?

HENRIETTA: I don't know. ... I was frightened ...

CROSSE: Don't you believe it, Freddy. She fired in cold blood.

FREDDY notes blood on CROSSE's shirt at the shoulder.

FREDDY: Oh, Mr. Crosse, it is a shoulder wound. It doesn't look too serious. I'll call for an ambulance.

CROSSE: No use. Call Glumly, Glower and Whatsis-name ...

FREDDY: Glumly, Glower and Smith is a funeral parlor! Now I am confused. Excuse me, Mr. Crosse, are you alive or dead?

CROSSE: Dead, definitely dead.

FREDDY: A dead man speaks. This is one for the Book of World Records.

HENRIETTA: He was hit in the shoulder. He is not dead. Svengali is feeling sorry for himself.

The intercom buzzes. FREDDY pushes the button. The voice of the publisher EMIL HARTHAUSER is heard.

HARTHAUSER: Crosse! I want to see you immediately.

FREDDY: He is indisposed, sir.

HARTHAUSER: Has he been drinking?

FREDDY: He has imbibed a bullet.

HARTHAUSER: A bullet? What kind of drink is that?

FREDDY: It is—ah—hard stuff.

HARTHAUSER: I will be there momentarily.

Intercom clicks off.

CROSSE: Freddy, I need three aspirin tablets—make it four.

FREDDY: It will take a while. The nearest drug store is on Lex.

CROSSE: Go.

FREDDY leaves.

HENRIETTA: You should go to a hospital.

CROSSE: This my accustomed place. The Emperor, otherwise known as Emil Harthauser, will expect to find me here.

CROSSE lays his head on the desk. Enter HAR-THAUSER. He nudges CROSSE.

HARTHAUSER: So drunk, he can't wake up. That's the last straw! Crosse, turn your notes on Zachariah over to Krystal Kracker. She will replace you.

HENRIETTA: Who is Krystal Kracker?

HARTHAUSER: She is—

CROSSE: —a pain in the ass!

HARTHAUSER: I will not respond to a drunk's provocation. [To HENRIETTA] Krystal is my special assistant. Brilliant, thinks like a man. [A second look at HENRIETTA] Are you employed here?

HENRIETTA: I am a visitor. My name is Henrietta.

HARTHAUSER: I have met you before.

HENRIETTA: My full name is Henrietta Zachariah.

HARTHAUSER: Zach— Are you related to the City's Controller?

HENRIETTA: I am his wife.

HARTHAUSER: I regret to say it, but your husband is fleecing the city. I am determined to expose him.

HENRIETTA: Why him? You could start with the mayor.

HARTHAUSER: Zachariah is obnoxious—a crook with a snooty attitude.

HENRIETTA: He contradicted you in the mayor's office. That should have been a lesson to you: have your facts straight before you speak.

HARTHAUSER: Zachariah's purpose was to embarrass me. I put him in his place. He is corrupt: you could see it in his face. I put my senior editor in charge of the investigation and look at him.

HENRIETTA: All you have come up with are rumors and sickening headlines—nothing substantial. My husband is innocent.

HARTHAUSER: In this city, there is no such thing as an innocent politician. Every one of them has something to hide. A journalist has to be a bulldog: sniff it out, then rip it out. That is my slogan: sniff it out, then rip it out. ... While Crosse sleeps, Krystal will get the job done.

HENRIETTA: I want to persuade you to call off the bulldog named Krystal.

HARTHAUSER: Persuade me! Not likely.

HENRIETTA: I own fifty-one percent of this corporation's stock.

HARTHAUSER: [**Startled, losing steam**] The person who owns fifty-one percent is an old and dear friend of mine, Eugenia Clark.

HENRIETTA: She passed away.

HARTHAUSER: She did! Of all things. She should have let me know.

HENRIETTA: Eugenia was my aunt. I inherited.

HARTHAUSER: I see. You think that your fifty-one percent entitles you to run the paper. Stockholder revolts are slow: it will take years to get rid of me. By that time I will have moved on. I will be a senator. I plan to run, you know. All the right people want me to do it. The Presidency will be in my sights. ... Fifty-one percent, eh. When I am gone you will have my job. In 1932—ten years from now—you can cover the story of my ascent to the Presidency. [Studies HENRIETTA] We have met before. Where?

HENRIETTA: At your daughter's coming-out party.

HARTHAUSER: Which daughter?

HENRIETTA: The wallflower.

HARTHAUSER: Phoebe. Ah, yes, looking at you now it seems to have been yesterday. You and I had an intimate chat.

HENRIETTA: I was the other wallflower in the room. You came on like a German tank. I was backed up against a wall.

As he talks, HARTHAUSER moves in on HENRIETTA. She retreats.

HARTHAUSER: My ancestry is not German, it is a mix of French and Dutch. The Dutch side appreciates great art, the French side appreciates fine foods and the feminine mystique. And you, my dear are a fine specimen of the latter. ... Phoebe's coming-out party: all the social butterflies were fluttering about, but you stood out.

There was something magical about you—your eyes. I was drawn to you, slowly, gingerly ...

Her back to the wall, HENRIETTA can retreat no further. HARTHAUSER fondles her, tries to kiss her. BANG! A shot is heard.

HARTHAUSER: Ouch! ... Was that a firecracker?

HENRIETTA: It was my way of saying back off.

HARTHAUSER: Is there a bee in the room? [**Looks about**] I don't see him. ... A bee sting hurts, but it is nothing serious. No harm done. All is right with me. [**Looks about, perplexed**] Something is wrong with the world. ... It seems to be leaving me. ... Oh! There is a trolley. I must catch it, find a seat.

HARTHAUSER staggers about the room. Like the ball in a pinball machine, he ricochets off furniture and walls. He ends up on a chair in front of a wall.

HARTHAUSER: [**Breathless**] I just made it—the trolley. ... Where is it going? ... Ah, a destination sign: Nowhere. A trolley to Nowhere? ... Probably a suburb. ... What is happening to me? ... My insides are dissolving away. ... This can't be! Greatness awaits me. I have friends in the right places. I am destined to be elected President.

KRYSTAL KRACKER enters. She is austere, strides like a soldier.

KRYSTAL: What is going on? ... Mr. Harthauser! Are you alright?

HARTHAUSER: I don't know. I feel no pain—except for the bee sting. ... It is odd, but I feel empty, a hide with nothing inside riding a trolley to nowhere.

KRYSTAL: Come, sir, it is an attack of the vapors. You will be alright.

HARTHAUSER: A suit of skin, nothing within ...

KRYSTAL becomes aware of HENRIETTA, who speaks first.

HENRIETTA: Are you Krystal?

KRYSTAL: Krystal Kracker, special assistant to Mr. Harthauser. Who are you?

HENRIETTA: I am Henrietta Zachariah.

KRYSTAL: Related to Roderick?

HENRIETTA: His wife.

KRYSTAL: What happened to Mr. Harthauser?

HENRIETTA: I shot him. It was self-defense. He was about to rape me.

HARTHAUSER: She lies ... lies ...

CROSSE: Shot me in cold blood ...

KRYSTAL: Crosse, too? ... You are having a good day, aren't you? Enjoy it while you can, your future is not very bright. Do you really expect a jury to believe that you shot two men in self-defense? You will join your husband in jail. Yesterday I interviewed a man who Crosse overlooked. He has documents that will incriminate your husband. **[Through clenched teeth]** I will nail both of you!

KRYSTAL turns to face HARTHAUSER.

KRYSTAL: Come, Mr. H, let me help you.

BANG!

KRYSTAL: Ouch! ... Is there a bee in the room? ... No bee that I can see. ... Oh! The room is moving. The whole room is revolving. ... I hear music. ...

KRYSTAL's staggering is that of a ballet dancer. She ends up in the chair next to HARTHAUSER and flops her head on his shoulder.

HARTHAUSER: Get off my shoulder.

KRYSTAL and HARTHAUSER take turns flopping heads on shoulders. Finally KRYSTAL moves over one seat.

KRYSTAL: My insides are emptying out. Little needles all over my body ...

HARTHAUSER: A suit of skin, nothing within ...

CROSSE: [Sits up, yawns, stands] We dead awaken.

KRYSTAL: Dead! What are you talking about?

CROSSE: There is a simple explanation. We were struck by metaphysical bullets—also known as Buddhist bullets.

HARTHAUSER: Metaphysical bullets!

KRYSTAL: Buddhist bullets! Buddhism and bullets are incompatible.

CROSSE: A British archaeologist—name of Hawkins—worked in Tibet while I was there. On one occasion—it was during a celebration honoring the Dalai Lama—he made a remark that the Lama took to be an insult. The next day Hawkins was struck by a bullet. He thought he was stung by a bee. [To HENRIETTA] Where did you get that pistol?

HENRIETTA: Aunt Eugenia bought it from a man in India. She told me to keep it in my purse: it would give me self-confidence.

CROSSE: Has it improved your self-confidence?

HENRIETTA: Now that I have used it, yes.

CROSSE: May I see it?

HENRIETTA hands the pistol to CROSSE. He examines it.

KRYSTAL: You have the pistol, Crosse. Shoot her!

CROSSE: I was about to fall in love with a lady who trusted me. But she didn't trust me: this odd gun holds just three bullets. Too bad. I wanted to see what a metaphysical bullet looked like.

CROSSE hands the pistol to HENRIETTA.

HARTHAUSER: What the deuce is a metaphysical bullet?

CROSSE: It is a compound of elements not known to science. You die, but you retain a memory of life—physical and mental.

HARTHAUSER: I won't die. The wound is superficial.

KRYSTAL: So is mine.

CROSSE: No medicine will cure you. We three will die. But we are given a chance to arrive at our personal truth—our karma—before the lights go out. Before Hawkins died he said that he had glimpsed Nirvana, that it was worth dying for. His last words were: "Crosse, you will one day be stung by a bee." I forgot those words—until I felt the sting.

HARTHAUSER: A bee sting! That is what I felt.

KRYSTAL: So did I.

CROSSE: The wound is trivial, but it is a death sentence. You feel a certain hollowness—I feel it now. The world is moving strangely.

HARTHAUSER: End station: Nowhere. I have to get off this trolley.

HARTHAUSER steps forward.

KRYSTAL: You rode a trolley to nowhere. My world is spinning, slowly ejecting me. ... Crosse might be right. Karma ... Nirvana... my only hope ...

HARTHAUSER: I can believe in a bee and a bullet; Karma is a crackpot notion, Nirvana is nonsense.

CROSSE: This is not ordinary dying. It is a migration into another phase of existence.

HARTHAUSER: You won't find it. It doesn't exist. A newspaper man should know that.

CROSSE: A newspaper man—

KRYSTAL: I would prefer it if you would say newspaper person.

CROSSE: Very well. A newspaper person set on telling the truth is preferable to one who is looking for scandal.

HARTHAUSER: Truth is for the back pages; sports and scandal sell newspapers. Al Capone pays our bonuses, Babe Ruth pays the electric bills.

KRYSTAL: You have got it right, Mr. H.

CROSSE: Kracker, you are no longer required to parrot Harthauser. You don't have to flatter anyone. That is one of the very few advantages of being dead.

KRYSTAL: I didn't think of that. I can reveal things I keep bottled up inside me. I am a student of Eastern religions. My guru says that step one on the path to Nirvana is to unburden one's self, tell people what you really think of them. You, Crosse, are talented—I give you that—but you are insufferable. As for you, Mr. H, you are a self-centered, egotistical, overbearing—

HENRIETTA: —German tank.

KRYSTAL: A perfect metaphor! [Addresses HARTHAUSER] You are not well-liked. The board of directors wants to get rid of you. They want me to replace you.

HARTHAUSER: Unfortunately for the board members Eugenia's fifty-one percent was on my side. I knew about the plot: I am shocked to hear that you were their partner. ... Suppose you succeeded. What would you do?

KRYSTAL: Under my direction, the *Gazette* would advance the cause of women.

HARTHAUSER: You would despoil the pages of the *Gazette* with feminist rant! That is heresy!

KRYSTAL: I am a feminist—a secret feminist.

HARTHAUSER: That is treason! If you had your way, I suppose that Sanger woman would have a daily column.

KRYSTAL: Margaret Sanger: I speak her name reverentially. I am her disciple.

HARTHAUSER: That woman is a threat to social order! And you are her follower! What is this world coming to?

KRYSTAL: The world is a man-made mess. If Margaret Sanger has her way, women will join men to create a better world.

CROSSE: More likely an even worse mess.

HARTHAUSER: You have deceived me, Krystal.

KRYSTAL: Deception is necessary. Your rule is oppressive.

HARTHAUSER: What about you, Crosse? Is my rule oppressive?

CROSSE: It is not your rule that oppresses me, it is your aggressive journalistic style. Rip-it-out journalism is masculine. Journalism, at its best, is a feminine art. Journalism's goddess—my goddess—is a lady of easy virtue. She traffics with gangsters, pimps, bawds and burglars as well as cops, politicians, archbishops and millionaires. She loves gossip. A hundred artfully written words become a hundred million spoken words as the story spreads through the city.

KRYSTAL: That is the worst possible philosophy! Gossips are idlers, immature human beings. This goddess you described is a whore—a totally degraded woman. Humanity has a mission: it is to create a just world. Journalists should lead the way.

CROSSE: [**Serious, stern**] With that attitude you will end up distorting the truth.

KRYSTAL: We will reveal the Real Truth: that which underlies appearances.

CROSSE: The Real Truth will turn out to be Your Opinion. Emil's philosophy and mine—much as we differ—accept the fact that corruption in the world is a fact of life. You are talking about an ideal world.

KRYSTAL: An improved world.

CROSSE: If we were stuck in some purified world, we would realize that the world we live in, with its vanities, its vices, its wars, its woes—and its glories—is the best of all possible worlds. It is a vigorous, passionate world. A utopia can never produce a Caravaggio or a Beethoven. [**CROSSE turns to HENRIETTA.**] ... By the way, Henrietta, you said that Freddy need not worry about me firing him. What was that about?

HARTHAUSER: She inherited Eugenia's fifty-one percent.

CROSSE: Fifty-one percent! I congratulate you. This is the most efficient corporate takeover ever. Now that you have eliminated the existing regime, you will run the newspaper.

KRYSTAL: She won't run the *Gazette*. You forget Crosse, that—when we die—she will have three murders to answer for.

CROSSE: That is a problem, isn't it? ... A question: has murder been committed? I say no: the wounds are trifling. Henrietta was not aware of the bullets' fatal potential. ... Still, three corpses would be an embarrassment. Henrietta must go on: her life is a destiny. She will continue marching in this comically sad, sadly comical parade known as life on an out-of-the-way spinning sphere called Earth. In the vast universe, this earth is a speck of dust; yet she harbors life, a cosmic phenomenon of the first magnitude.

A heavy fist hits the door. It flies open. LOVIE enters.

CROSSE: Lovie! How did you know that I need you?

LOVIE: I have an appointment to see you.

CROSSE: I forgot. What is it about?

LOVIE: I got the info you needed. It's enough to hang the poor bastard.

HENRIETTA: Oh!

HARTHAUSER: Who? Zachariah?

LOVIE: Naw, Cropsey, the police commissioner.

CROSSE: Thanks for everything, Lovie, but I will no longer need your information.

LOVIE: I spent good money to dig it up.

CROSSE: There is no time to explain, Lovie, but you will have to sell it to another paper. Did you bring your men with you?

LOVIE: I got two guys down the hall.

CROSSE: I am resigned to my fate. I feel no bitterness, no anger. Henrietta will run the *Gazette*. Here's the situation, Lovie: if Henrietta is to get the job done without police interference, three corpses need to disappear.

LOVIE: For you, Mr. Crosse, no charge. Where are the bodies?

CROSSE: This is not easy to explain, Lovie. All I ask is that you follow my instructions. Give me a shoulder to lean on and lead me down the street to the Benares restaurant.

LOVIE: The boodist place?

CROSSE: Yes. Seat me in the twilight corner opposite the portal that leads to Nirvana. Put a stiff drink in front of me—the usual—and I will contemplate Nirvana. There are two others to join me: Mr. Harthauser and Miss Kracker. Maybe your boys would lend them a hand. [**Addresses HARTHAUSER, KRYSTAL**] Are you two ready?

HARTHAUSER: I left the trolley to nowhere. As long as you are going somewhere, I might as well go. Still, it is peculiar ... very peculiar. ... The presidency ... Let it go. I will go with you.

KRYSTAL: I will stay. My dead body will convict her.

CROSSE: No jury will convict a woman who acted in desperation to save her husband. Even if she were sent to jail, all you would get from it is vengeance. What is that next to Nirvana?

KRYSTAL: Why are you so eager to protect this woman?

CROSSE: I have fallen in love with her. She is the most beautiful woman I have ever met. As for you, Krystal you would be wise to join me and Emil. Revenge is a negative passion! It embitters the soul.

KRYSTAL: Nirvana: the extinction of desire ... a cold, perpetual dream. ... I will go with you.

HENRIETTA: Julian—bon voyage.

CROSSE: Good luck to you, Henrietta. You will need it more than I will. ... We are ready, Lovie.

LOVIE: Sure, Mr. Crosse. I'll take you. My boys will help your friends.

Lights down slowly as CROSSE leans on LOVIE. They walk out the door.

ACT TWO

SCENE ONE

Four months later. HENRIETTA is seated at the desk that still has Crosse's name plate. She is editing news copy. FREDDY enters.

FREDDY: I brought you coffee, Henrietta.

HENRIETTA: Sit down, Freddy. I want to talk to you. [Freddy sits] You are very kind to run my errands. Why do you do it?

FREDDY: I am not trying to butter you up. I wouldn't do that for anyone. You are going through a lot. I am trying to help. ... I am sorry about your husband. Mr. Williams put his story on page eight. We kept it low key.

HENRIETTA: The *Telegraph* and the *World* were like vultures feasting on the carcass of a fallen man. To see front-page pictures of Roderick in handcuffs broke my heart. He was angry that I did not support him in the *Gazette*. As his wife I believed him; as a newspaper editor, I had doubts. I think thoughts now that once were inconceivable.

FREDDY: Do you still doubt your husband's guilt?

HENRIETTA: Yes. We decide guilt or innocence based on very simple criteria: such facts as attorneys have seized upon, testimony that witnesses are willing to reveal, concealing the rest. If we knew how to read the hearts of the accused and the accusers, justice would produce different verdicts.

FREDDY: If you were a juror how would you have voted?

HENRIETTA: A wife cannot testify against her husband—not even hypothetically. What about you—if you were on the jury?

FREDDY: Guilty. The facts were against him.

HENRIETTA: A fact is but the surface of a passion. We see the fact, we surmise the passion. Our surmise depends on how we are disposed: guilty or innocent.

FREDDY: Five years isn't bad: he will be out in two and a half. It won't be miserable: the politicians' jail is like a hotel.

> Self-absorbed, HENRIETTA articulates thoughts that normally would not be spoken.

HENRIETTA: A phase of my life has ended. I am now indifferent to my husband's fate. Is that proper for a woman? Politics ruined a good man—the father of our children.

They bear his name. So do I. I loved him, I was loyal to him. As a newspaper woman I must be loyal to no one. Julian Crosse was loyal to no one. To be indifferent to all persons and things: how easy for him, how hard for me. ... In the end, he was not indifferent to me. He wished me well. ... Why does a life work out the way it does? ...

HENRIETTA is absorbed in thought.

FREDDY: A penny for your thoughts.

HENRIETTA: I was thinking of what might have been. **[Snaps out of her reverie]** We must deal with the present: the *Gazette's* financial situation. Have you seen this week's circulation figures?

FREDDY: Same as last week and the week before.

HENRIETTA: Twenty percent lower than it used to be. We have repudiated Emil Harthauser's rip-it-out philosophy, but we must admit that he knew how to sell newspapers. Advertising revenue is down. It is a good thing we had a cash reserve.

FREDDY: Mr. Harthauser was a fanatic about maintaining a cash reserve.

HENRIETTA: The reserve won't last forever. We will need another round of staff reductions and pay cuts.

FREDDY: We would have a strike. People are already talking union.

HENRIETTA: Any ideas?

FREDDY: Increase circulation. If I were a reporter, my byline would be Freddy Flash. The first thing I would do is interview America's most influential feminist, Margaret Sanger.

HENRIETTA: What story would you tell?

FREDDY: People know nothing about Margaret Sanger, yet they either love her or hate her. Who is this woman who evokes such passions? Answer that question on the front page—with a photo. She is in New York this week giving public lectures.

HENRIETTA: Freddy, I hereby appoint you reporter. Interview Margaret Sanger.

FREDDY: I will need a photographer—maybe Paul Krieger.

HENRIETTA: Take Paul with you.

FREDDY: I am on my way.

FREDDY dashes off.

SCENE TWO

Lights down. Lights back up suggest a passage of time. HENRIETTA is still editing news stories. There is a knock at the door.

HENRIETTA: Come in.

The door opens, McGURK enters.

McGURK: Are you Harriet Zachariah?

HENRIETTA: No, I am not Harriet Zachariah.

McGURK: Well then, who are you?

HENRIETTA: Henrietta Zachariah.

McGURK: That is who I asked for.

HENRIETTA: You said Harriet.

McGURK: Oh. I have an aunt named Harriet.

HENRIETTA: Talk to her. I am busy.

McGURK: OK, that is enough of name games. My name is McGurk—James McGurk. I am a detective, New York Police Department.

McGURK shows HENRIETTA his ID. She studies it.

McGURK: Look, Mrs.— Henrietta. I want to ask you a few questions.

HENRIETTA: I have been asked a thousand questions. Do you have new ones?

McGURK: Maybe I do. There is a mystery for which one link in a chain of evidence is missing. That link most certainly involves a person. The question is, which person? Let me summarize.

McGURK's manner of speaking, like his pacing, appears casual, but is quite deliberate.

McGURK: Four months ago, three bodies were found seated side by side in a dark corner of the Benares restaurant. Witnesses said they were engaged in conversation for at least four hours. They recited prayers that no one understood. At times they were solemn; at other times they were like people at a revival meeting, clapping hands, laughing—even cheering. At last they laid their heads on the table and slept. They did not wake up. All three were members of the *Gazette*'s staff. All three had a bullet in them. The bullets were small: the coroner nearly missed them. The wounds were superficial: none should have been fatal—unless the bullets contained a poison. Autopsies revealed no *known* poison. The bullets fit no known gun. Did they shoot each other? Impossible—at least while they were in the restaurant. Gunshots would have been heard. They must have been shot before they came in. People with a bullet in them don't usually engage in a lively four-hour conversation. The whole thing is a puzzle—maybe even a perfect crime. ... I was wondering if you could shed any light on this problem.

HENRIETTA: The police and the district attorney's staff have questioned me to the point of exhaustion. I have nothing to add to the testimony I gave them.

McGURK: Hard evidence is lacking: thus, we must consider motives. You stood to gain by these deaths. Three top people die, and you take over.

HENRIETTA: I didn't gain a thing. I am a majority owner of this paper. I am running things until we can recruit a chief editor. I will then return to private life.

McGURK: I wonder if I might have a look around your office.

HENRIETTA: Not without a search warrant.

McGURK: I don't mean a thorough search. I just want to get a feel for this space.

HENRIETTA: Why?

McGURK: I have a feeling that the shootings took place in this office.

HENRIETTA: This office has been searched from top to bottom by the police. There is no justification for another search.

McGURK: Might I see the contents of your purse.

HENRIETTA: Why my purse?

McGURK: Weapons are sometimes concealed in purses.

HENRIETTA: I should demand a warrant, but you may have a look.

McGURK searches the purse and hands it back to HENRIETTA.

McGURK: Benares—I looked it up: it is a Buddhist holy city in India. At the restaurant, they talk a lot about reincarnation—that kind of stuff. Crosse ate there a lot and drank twice as much as he ate. Did he believe that spiritual stuff?

HENRIETTA: He told me that he did.

McGURK: It is of interest that this strange phenomenon occurred the day you visited Crosse. It didn't happen another day, but that particular day. You met in this office.

HENRIETTA: I was hoping to persuade Mr. Crosse to be fair to my husband in his press coverage.

McGURK: Persuade. One way to persuade someone is to aim a gun at him.

HENRIETTA: Reason, common sense—and charm— usually work better.

McGURK: Nothing intimidates more than a lethal weapon.

HENRIETTA: How about the fear of Hell.

McGURK: [**A heavy, exasperated sigh**] Let's get back to your interview with Crosse. Did he agree to let up on your husband?

HENRIETTA: I have answered that question at least a dozen times. The answer is no.

McGURK: You admitted to being angry.

HENRIETTA: I had good reason to be angry.

McGURK: Anger is a motive. You were the one person with motive and opportunity.

HENRIETTA: Detective McGurk, cops and attorneys have asked me all these questions. It is all on record. I thought that the District Attorney had closed the case.

McGURK: The DA decided that it was a group-suicide. They shoot each other in an alley outside the Benares, get rid of the gun, and enter the restaurant. Buddhism, nirvana, reincarnation: people with ideas like that figure they can start over. It sounds plausible, but I am not sold on the suicide theory. [McGURK deliberates upon an idea.] Do you suppose it is possible to die twice?

HENRIETTA: Good heavens! What inspired that thought?

McGURK: If they were wounded here, they would have gone to a hospital, not a restaurant. If they died—or were close to death—their bodies could have been taken to Benares. If they somehow revived at the restaurant and lived four more hours, the whole thing would make sense.

HENRIETTA: Do you suppose anyone would believe that?

McGURK: In this case we have to think of extraordinary possibilities.

HENRIETTA: In this world, the only things that are true are things people are willing to believe. Dying twice is not a popular idea.

McGURK: [A deep, exasperated breath] This is an irrational crime. Do you think there is a rational explanation for it?

HENRIETTA: I have no idea.

McGURK: Do you have any suggestions?

HENRIETTA: None.

McGURK: Do you have anything else to say?

HENRIETTA: Good luck.

McGURK: I hope you won't repeat that notion I had—dying twice.

HENRIETTA: When I speak to the district attorney I will treat it as a joke.

McGURK: There is no need to talk to him.

HENRIETTA: He told me that, if anything unusual happens, I am to call him.

McGURK: You are a smart lady, Henrietta. You are the kind of woman who knows more than she talks about. There aren't many of them around.

HENRIETTA: Do you have any more questions? If not, I have work to do.

McGURK: Good day.

McGURK exits, HENRIETTA resumes her work.

SCENE THREE

FREDDY is ending his interview with MARGARET SANGER.

FREDDY: Thank you Mrs. Sanger. You have been generous with your time. I have one more question.

SANGER: That is all the time I can spare. Where did your photographer go?

FREDDY: He is back at the shop developing his pictures.

SANGER: I hope it will be a decent photo.

FREDDY: Paul is an excellent—and honest—photographer.

SANGER: I am frequently misrepresented in the press.

FREDDY: That is a price a reformer must pay.

SANGER: I explain my position on the family and the news story says that I am anti-family.

FREDDY: [Consults his notes] You told me that you were pro-family with the understanding that the relationship between husband and wife would change. A woman would not turn her back on her husband; rather, because she has learned how to prevent conception until she wants to conceive, she can enjoy sex as much as he does.

SANGER: Another slander is that I am a man-hater.

FREDDY: You said that you wished to end male-domination.

SANGER: Another way to put that is that I wish to improve women's rights. My mother brought ten children into the world and died at age fifty. If she had known how to prevent conception, her life would have been much better.

FREDDY: If your mother took your advice, you might not have been born.

SANGER: I would rather that my mother be happy without me than miserable with me.

FREDDY: You would sacrifice your life for the happiness of another.

SANGER: Let's not go into that.

FREDDY: The story I want to tell is your personal story. Your struggle has been hard. Your success is undeniable. You have found numerous ways to promote your cause. You publish pamphlets, organize demonstrations and make speeches. You stare down the bullies who threaten you with sticks and bricks.

SANGER: I try, by my example, to give women the confidence to stand up for their own interests.

FREDDY: Pamphlets, speeches, demonstrations: which is most effective?

SANGER: Getting arrested beats all of them. It gets you lots of free press.

FREDDY: Can I quote you?

SANGER: Yes, quote me.

SANGER exits. FREDDY scribbles a note on his pad and exits.

SCENE FOUR

HENRIETTA is reading letters. FREDDY enters with a sack of letters and sets it on the floor.

FREDDY: More letters to the editor. We are setting a record.

HENRIETTA: I don't need to read any more, Freddy. Seventy percent of this is hate mail, thirty percent love mail. Lovers and haters alike buy a paper. Every newsstand copy was sold.

FREDDY: Margaret Sanger gave a lecture last night. She expected fifty people. As a result of our story, the lecture hall was packed. The neighboring streets were jammed with people wanting to get a glimpse of her. They installed exterior speakers so that people in the street could hear her speech. The whole neighborhood had to be closed off. I have got that story too. Mr. Williams will put it on page one, with two photos. And he will print twenty percent more copies.

HENRIETTA: You did a good job Freddy.

FREDDY: Mr. Crosse would not have thought so: he would have called it hagiography. I did not maintain enough distance between me and my subject. The result was too much of her point of view.

HENRIETTA: I had the same impression, but the story served a public information purpose; and it was a boost for the *Gazette*.

FREDDY: Mr. Crosse would have edited it, cut it in half, and put it on page four. It is not the newspaper's job—he said it often—to promote causes.

HENRIETTA: We must keep in mind that it is your first story; it is a huge success—and it is lifting the *Gazette* out of its doldrums. ... Poor editing, we sell papers ...

Pause. HENRIETTA is glum.

FREDDY: What about the Chief Editor's doldrums?

HENRIETTA: I have been wondering about me. What do you think of me, Freddy?

FREDDY: You are a good angel, a breath of fresh air in these offices. The entire staff feels that way.

HENRIETTA: Once upon a time my life was simpler—and happier. Then one day I set out to correct what I thought was an injustice. Three people died.

FREDDY: When my time comes, I would like to go the way they did. ... It is like a Greek tragedy where death is destiny.

HENRIETTA: That sounds nice—very poetic. But it is not convincing.

FREDDY: Mr. Crosse, Krystal and Mr. Harthauser had reason to go: the atmosphere they lived in was poisoned. They faced destiny bravely. They will try again.

HENRIETTA: Are you talking about reincarnation?

FREDDY: That is one way to put it. They were proto-types. A prototype has an ancestor and a successor.

HENRIETTA: Where do you get such big ideas? You didn't finish high school.

FREDDY: I got a lot of it from Mr. Crosse. He was a college education all by himself. He had me read the Greek tragedies and Shakespeare. I loved it.

Pause. HENRIETTA picks up a stack of resumes.

HENRIETTA: I have to get back to work. I am interviewing applicants for the chief editor job.

FREDDY: What will you do when you hire an editor?

HENRIETTA: I shall stay on for a month, then I am off to Tibet. I want to find out what Julian Crosse knew.

FREDDY: Don't bring the pistol.

HENRIETTA: **[An eye-popping response]** What pistol!!?

FREDDY: The one that doesn't exist. The one I shall not speak of again.

HENRIETTA smiles. FREDDY exits. Slow fade.

SCENE FIVE

An institutional lamp, a bare bulb. McGURK reads a letter he has written. His audience is a fellow detective, LOU, who wears a battered fedora and is seated downstage, his back to the audience.

McGURK: This is what I wrote. "Mr. District Attorney, I accept your reprimand for pursuing a case you had already closed. My action was improper." ... Should I say improper? Unfortunate might be a better word. ... No. Being unfortunate is like being unlucky: no one will bet on you. .... An error in judgement? ... No. A cop who admits to an error in judgement will be sent to Bellevue—a month locked up with those goofy psychiatrists. ... I'll stick with improper.

Reads

"My intentions were to serve you by clearing up a lingering doubt. I was guilty of excessive zeal, not insubordination. Accordingly, I ask that you reconsider your decision to suspend me without pay for sixty days. I have a wife and four children." That ought to get through to him: he has four kids. ... He also has a Park Avenue mistress.

Reads

"I pursued the matter because some questions remained unanswered. The person who complained to you, Henrietta Zachariah, is the wife of a convicted city official. I interviewed her because I was convinced that she knows more that she has disclosed. The interview confirmed that impression. The lady is smart—smarter than a lady is supposed to be. If this was a perfect crime, I felt certain that she was the key to it. She met Crosse the day of the shootings. She said she went home at the same time the three newspaper people left for the restaurant. Conveniently for her, three witnesses who might confirm her story, are dead. I did say that I didn't believe the group-suicide theory: that was an interrogation tactic. About dying twice, that was a joke. When all is said and done, your group-suicide theory prevails. It is supported by the fact that all three victims engaged in a long, friendly conversation before dying. It was a brilliant deduction. I have no reason to doubt it." ... That should butter him up.

Reads

"In conclusion, I hope that my long and honorable service will persuade you to reconsider my suspension.

Sincerely, James McGurk." ... I hope that will do. Stuck in an apartment with wife and kids for sixty days will drive me crazy.

McGURK folds the letter into an envelope, then thinks a moment.

McGURK: Henrietta has a newspaper on her side. Her weapons are words. They are deadlier than bullets. [Addresses LOU] What do you think, Lou: should I continue the fight?

LOU shakes his head, 'no.' McGURK tears up the letter.

McGURK: Sixty days! ... I'll call Lovie. Maybe I could drive one of his cabs.

McGURK and LOU exit. Lights down.

SCENE SIX

Lights up on HENRIETTA at her desk. There is a knock at the door.

HENRIETTA: Come in.

KATRINA CROWLEY enters and hands her resume to HENRIETTA. She is the image of Krystal Kracker, but girlish. HENRIETTA stares at KATRINA.

HENRIETTA: Katrina Crowley. Do people call you Kate?

KATRINA: I prefer Katrina.

HENRIETTA: You are single—

KATRINA: I have had my fishhook in the pond for ten years. No bites.

HENRIETTA: The pond in Akron, Ohio, is no doubt small—and provincial. ... I am Henrietta.

KATRINA: Are you the Chief Editor?

HENRIETTA: Yes.

KATRINA: I didn't expect that a woman would be interviewing me.

HENRIETTA: Are you disappointed?

KATRINA: Not a bit. I was delighted to see the Margaret Sanger story you ran.

HENRIETTA: There will be another front page story tomorrow.

KATRINA: I can't wait to see it.

HENRIETTA: Are you a feminist?

KATRINA: I took my mother's advice: two cheers for feminism, not three.

HENRIETTA: Have you decided to move to New York even if we don't hire you?

KATRINA: Yes. Bigger pond.

HENRIETTA: Your resume speaks for itself. Let's talk about you. How do you see yourself?

KATRINA: [Puzzled by the odd question] I don't know. If there is one thing you don't see, it is yourself.

HENRIETTA: When you look in the mirror, what do you see?

> Katrina plainly resents the question, but decides to answer it.

KATRINA: Until I was seventeen, I cried.

HENRIETTA: I am sorry. That was not a fair question.

HENRIETTA stares at KATRINA.

KATRINA: Is something wrong with me? You ask me what I think of myself, you look at me strangely—

HENRIETTA: Excuse me, I was distraught. ... You are with the Star, Akron, Ohio. Eight years altogether, three years in your present job. How do you get on with your colleagues?

KATRINA: That is another odd question. ... There, you have done it again: looked at me in that peculiar way.

HENRIETTA: I am sorry—I didn't intend it. It is just that you are a picture-image of a lady who used to work here.

KATRINA: Krystal Kracker: I saw her picture in the paper. People thought it was me. I thought it was me.

HENRIETTA: Krystal was a very different person from you.

KATRINA: What was she like?

HENRIETTA: She was a strong personality—militant, ambitious.

KATRINA: [**Excited, gossipy**] Is that why she was shot? Was it you? ... Oh! I should not have asked that question.

HENRIETTA: Apparently you have entertained that possibility.

KATRINA: If you told me you did it, I would not repeat it. Oh! There I go again. ... My tongue sometimes runs faster than my brain. ... Have I blown the interview?

HENRIETTA: Not yet. I see that you have direct sales experience. Were you good at it?

KATRINA: The best. I would call business people and get them to buy advertising space. I always exceeded my quotas. On the phone I am a charmer.

HENRIETTA scribbles a note on her business card, attaches it to KATRINA's resume, and hands it to her.

HENRIETTA: Go down the hall to the receptionist. She will tell you where Ben Friedman's office is. He is in charge of advertising. Hand him my card with your resume. Talk to him about the direct sales opening. On your way, would you inform the gentleman in the waiting room that I can see him now.

KATRINA: Mr. Thorne. We had quite a chat. We agreed that we like New York, though he does not look the type. [**Giggles**] Denim jacket, cowboy boots, string tie, cowboy hat. He is from the *real* West—Wyoming. [**Frowns**] He could use better manners. He has met me for the first time and tells me that he wouldn't hire me for any job. Can you imagine! If I were you I would not hire him.

HENRIETTA: Ben Friedman is easy to get along with. Don't blow it.

KATRINA: Ben Friedman, direct sales opening, resume, Henrietta's card, don't blow it. I've got it. Bye.

KATRINA exits.

SCENE SEVEN

A few moments pass. JARRET THORNE enters and sets his hat on a chair. He bears a striking resemblance to Julian Crosse.

HENRIETTA: Eek! This is spooky! Is Nirvana catching up with me? I just interviewed a woman who was a picture-image of Krystal Kracker.

THORNE: And I am a picture-image of Julian Crosse. Well almost: I am a quarter inch taller and five years younger than Julian.

HENRIETTA: Jarret Thorne. Your last name has an 'e' on the end.

THORNE: Crosse's name had an 'e' on the end. Is there a reason you haven't taken down his name plate?

HENRIETTA: No reason. ... I take it that you knew Mr. Crosse.

THORNE: I got to know him at editor conventions. People took us to be twins.

HENRIETTA: Did you and he get along?

THORNE: I liked Julian. He had a first-rate mind. World-weary humor: it was genuine. He once took a trip out west: I entertained him for three days. The Rocky Mountains did not impress him. He preferred the Himalayas: they were good Buddhists. ... Julian's final passage was strange. I wonder if it was what he secretly wanted.

HENRIETTA: How did you rate Julian—Mr. Crosse—as a journalist?

THORNE: There wasn't a better newspaper man anywhere. He stressed factual accuracy. He would not accept ambiguity or journalistic spin. He told me about his newspaper work—in New York, in this office. I was fascinated. The variety of good and evil in this city in one week is more than we get in a whole year. If we get one murder in a month, we count ourselves lucky.

HENRIETTA: Lucky! The corpse isn't lucky.

THORNE: Murder sells papers. Some people would call the newspaper man's view cynical, even amoral. We redeem ourselves by keeping society informed.

HENRIETTA: You are prepared to leave your present job: are you dissatisfied with it?

THORNE: I am very satisfied with my present job. I am willing to leave it only for Julian's job.

HENRIETTA: [Consults THORNE's resume] I don't need to ask you about your experience: you have done it all, from delivery boy to chief editor. I would like to know Jarret Thorne, the man.

THORNE: I am a Wyoming boy—the son of Jack Thorne. I am more successful than my father, though he was as good a man as any. Mom left Dad when I was a child. She moved in with her family. I would visit her—stay a week or two, then drift off. Dad wouldn't divorce her. He was old-fashioned—didn't believe in divorce.

HENRIETTA: [Checks resume] You were twice divorced—

THORNE: Dad was shocked, threatened to disown me—but he didn't do it. I get along with my ex-wives—more or less.

HENRIETTA: You have three children ...

THORNE: My daughter is in high school. My son is in Boston studying journalism. A son by my first wife works the family farm.

HENRIETTA: You are chief editor at a small-town newspaper. How would you run a New York paper?

THORNE: The same way as I do the small-town paper. I am friendly with subordinates, but I don't socialize with them. I insist on quality writing and meeting deadlines. I set editorial policy: some papers have a committee doing that. I detest committees.

HENRIETTA: We had a committee: Julian ignored it. They tried a comeback when I took the job. They forgot that I am a majority owner: I dissolved the committee.

THORNE: [Laughs] Good job. ... I take it that you set editorial policy.

HENRIETTA: I do.

THORNE: The front page story on Margaret Sanger in today's edition is not the sort of thing Julian would have allowed.

HENRIETTA: We did it just this once. It gave circulation a much needed boost.

THORNE: The boost will be short-lived. There are other ways to boost circulation. When dealing with political issues, a newspaper must remain neutral. Another thing: the Freddy Flash byline is amateurish.

HENRIETTA: I guess my inexperience showed. That is why I am recruiting my own replacement.

THORNE: Keep the job. In a year you will be the best in the business.

HENRIETTA: I want to get back to being a rich society lady.

THORNE: Idle rich! After what you have been through, will that satisfy you?

HENRIETTA: We rich are not idle. We do a good deal for charity, education and diplomacy. Art museums, operas and symphony orchestras would not exist without us.

THORNE: [Studies Henrietta] You won't be able to go back to it.

HENRIETTA: Really! What is to stop me?

THORNE: There is nothing to stop you except yourself. Here you are in the hectic world of journalism, running a big-city newspaper. I followed Julian's story closely. I published every dispatch. We called it the Buddhist Suicide Club. I can't explain it, but you were the most fascinating person in the story.

HENRIETTA: My name was hardly mentioned.

THORNE: That adds to the mystery. **[Studies HENRIETTA]** You are a changed person: I would bet on it. My guess is that a single event transformed you: the encounter with Julian Crosse.

HENRIETTA: Transformed! How would you know that? You just met me.

THORNE: I see it, I hear it. You have the expression of a poker-player—a good one.

HENRIETTA: I have never played poker.

THORNE: I am talking about the game of life.

HENRIETTA: Odd that you should say that. My daughter, age seven, told me that I am not the mommy I used to be. She is right. I am now playing the game of life; in the past, I watched life from the sidelines. I was amused by the world, afraid of its rough parts.

THORNE: Does your daughter prefer the old mommy?

HENRIETTA: Unfortunately, yes.

THORNE: She'll get over it.

HENRIETTA: I hope so.

THORNE: There is a question that was not answered—at least not in the news dispatches. You had an interview with Julian. You did not get what you wanted from him. Were you angry?

HENRIETTA: The District Attorney asked me that question. My answer was yes, I was angry, very angry. I threatened to take my story to another newspaper.

THORNE: Did the DA buy it?

HENRIETTA: Buy what?

THORNE: Taking your story to another newspaper.

HENRIETTA: Of course he did. It was true.

THORNE: How did Julian react?

HENRIETTA: He brushed me off. He was so smug. I felt like a nonentity.

THORNE: You must have been terribly frustrated.

HENRIETTA: I was furious.

THORNE: Did Julian appeal to you—at a deeper level of feeling?

HENRIETTA: That is the oddest question I have been asked.

THORNE: It is the crucial question. Julian had a way with women. He wore the mask of a world-weary traveler through life. At a deeper level he sent out strong emotional vibes. Women—unconventional women—were attuned to that. An angry woman might shoot him, then keep his name plate in place.

HENRIETTA: Are you implying—

THORNE: I am not implying anything. I was thinking of possibilities. If a woman points a gun at a man he will plead for mercy or run for cover. Not Julian. For him it would be a test of his mastery. How did he deal with it? That would be his crucial moment.

HENRIETTA: You seem to be obsessed with the idea that a woman shot him.

THORNE: The bullet was small, the gun had to be small—the sort of weapon that would fit into a woman's purse.

HENRIETTA: Do you think I shot him?

THORNE: To be candid—a newspaper man has candor in his bones: I wouldn't rule you out.

HENRIETTA: [**Irritated**] Rule-in, rule-out. What is the point of that? The matter is settled. The district attorney decided that it was group-suicide.

THORNE: I published that story. I didn't believe it, but it was a way to close out the case.

> Pause. HENRIETTA's expression is cold. She holds THORNE's eyes.

HENRIETTA: Stand up.

> THORNE complies.

HENRIETTA: Turn around. I want to see your back.

> THORNE turns around. BAM! HENRIETTA punches a staple into some papers. THORNE does not flinch. HENRIETTA arranges papers on her desk.

HENRIETTA: Face me again. ... Sit.

> THORNE complies.

THORNE: What was that about?

HENRIETTA: Nothing. I had a little filing to do.

Pause. A faint smile on his lips, THORNE studies HENRIETTA.

THORNE: May I ask a personal question?

HENRIETTA: I thought I was interviewing you.

THORNE: I believe you have me figured me out.

HENRIETTA: Why do you want to ask a personal question?

THORNE: I am a newspaper man. I have a natural curiosity about interesting people.

HENRIETTA: What is the personal question?

THORNE: Were you happily married?

HENRIETTA: Julian asked if my husband loved me.

THORNE: A good journalist gets right to the heart of the matter. Did you answer his question?

HENRIETTA: No.

THORNE: Would you answer my question?

HENRIETTA deliberates.

HENRIETTA: On my wedding day I took an oath for life. That was a way of saying I am happy now and will be happy ever more.

THORNE: Your husband spoke the same words. Apparently they had a different meaning for him. It came out during the trial that he had mistresses. Did you suspect him?

HENRIETTA: I was a good wife: I trusted my husband—until I saw him in Lord and Taylor, arm-in-arm with a woman who wasn't me. I thought of confronting them: the wallflower in me said don't do it. I hired a detective, Mr. Burke. He was quite efficient. The woman was an employee in Roderick's department. She is French: Genevieve Martin. Mr. Burke also found out that Genevieve left Roderick for Julian Crosse. That is when I decided to visit Mr. Crosse.

THORNE: And—

HENRIETTA: He swore that Genevieve was not giving him information about my husband. I can't say why, but I believed him.

THORNE: He had won you over.

HENRIETTA: That is nonsense.

THORNE: In our conversation, you have referred to him as Julian, not Crosse. The tone of your voice when you speak his name is, shall we say—

HENRIETTA: No need to say it. I get the point. I suppose that—in the end—I thought better of Julian.

THORNE: He got you to realize—admit to yourself—that your husband still had your loyalty, but not your heart.

HENRIETTA: [Skeptical, sarcastic] That is a remarkable insight made at a distance of two-thousand miles. Have you studied Freud?

THORNE: I have had experience falling in and out of love.

HENRIETTA: You assume that your experiences explain my experience. [A harsh tone] You are too presumptuous, Mr. Thorne.

THORNE: I have offended you. It was unintentional. I apologize.

HENRIETTA says nothing but holds THORNE's eyes. Her expression is cold. A tense silence. Pensive, THORNE comes to a decision.

THORNE: After the things I have said—personal things—it might be best if I withdrew my application.

HENRIETTA hands THORNE his resume.

THORNE: It was nice meeting you, Henrietta.

HENRIETTA says nothing. THORNE restores his hat to his head and walks slowly toward the door.

HENRIETTA: Do you want the job?

THORNE stops in his tracks.

THORNE: I had the distinct impression that I was dismissed.

HENRIETTA: Answer my question.

THORNE: [**Visibly swallowing his pride**] Am I to plead for it? ... Yes, dammit, I want the job.

HENRIETTA: How soon can you start?

THORNE: Whoa! Slow down Jarret, slow down. Do you want to work for a lady who is a better poker player than you are?

THORNE struggles with the decision. He is giving HENRIETTA a chance to make a conciliatory remark. She says nothing. THORNE is defeated.

THORNE: The lady has played her hand, I have played mine. She has a full house, I have a pair of eights.

THORNE laughs as he mimes the act of throwing cards on a table.

THORNE: I fold.

HENRIETTA: Are you still in the game?

THORNE: [Accepting defeat] Yes.

HENRIETTA: [Businesslike] When can I expect you?

THORNE: I have to settle things in Wyoming. Three day train ride each way. Give me fifteen days.

HENRIETTA checks desk calendar, counts days.

HENRIETTA: I'll expect you on the—

The door opens, HENRY HARDSTONE bursts upon the scene. He is an Emil Harthauser look-alike.

HARDSTONE: I am sorry to intrude, but I must speak to Henrietta.

HENRIETTA: [Astonished, spooked] Good heavens! I can't believe this! Who are you?

HARDSTONE: I am sorry. I didn't mean to startle you. I would have knocked, but I haven't the time. I am in a terrible hurry. My name is Henry Hardstone. I didn't pick the name, it picked me. I am not at all hard, and I am definitely not a stone. The receptionist told me to go to the waiting room. Everywhere I go they shift me off to the waiting room. I have been out of work for four months. I can no longer wait. No one will hire me because I am overqualified. I used to be a top executive, but I will take any work and do it well. I need to be gainfully employed. Can you help me?

HENRIETTA: I have no openings at the executive level.

HARDSTONE: I know how to work. I can find a way to like what I am doing.

HENRIETTA Writes a note on the back of a calling card and hands it to HARDSTONE.

HENRIETTA: Ask the receptionist to direct you to Jack Kearn. He is in charge of circulation. He has an opening for a dispatcher. Show him this note with your resume.

HARDSTONE: Jack Kearn. I am on my way. [Exits]

THORNE: Do you think he will be satisfied with a dispatcher job?

HENRIETTA: No, but it doesn't matter. He will work his way up the corporate ladder. After a long search, Henry Hardstone has arrived where he belongs—at the *Gazette*. He is a picture-image of Emil Harthauser; Katrina is a duplicate Krystal Kracker; you are the second coming of Julian Crosse. All this in one day! That cinches it: Nirvana is closing in on me! I must take a trip to Tibet and pay my respects. The Himalayas are said to be the world's most majestic mountain range.

THORNE: Try Wyoming instead. In Wyoming, you stand naked at the foot of the mountain: the mountain makes no promises—not to a man or woman; nor to the eagle that rides its turbulent winds; nor to the coyote or chipmunk, the owl or the skylark. Every creature knows precisely who he or she is. If you want to figure out who you are, that is the place to be.

HENRIETTA: Looking at you, I would swear that you are Julian Crosse. But your style—your outlook on life— is not at all like his.

THORNE: For all his cosmopolitan disillusionment— which he thoroughly enjoyed—Julian thought of life in capital letters: L-I-F-E. I spell it in lower case letters: life is a fact, no more than that.

HENRIETTA: Are you a fact? Am I?

THORNE: We are facts: millions of them, but facts nonetheless. The spirit of the world—if there be one—is embedded in facts. ... Are you dissatisfied with that?

HENRIETTA: It is not an appealing philosophy.

THORNE: You have hired me: now is the time to fire me.

HENRIETTA, at her desk calendar, counts days.

HENRIETTA: Fifteen days ... See you on the twenty-ninth. If you show up looking like a cowboy, you will get a bath in the East River. We begin punctually at nine.

THORNE: That will take some getting used to: in Wyoming, my work day starts at seven-thirty.

THORNE tips his hat and exits. A bemused lady, through tears and laughter, gives up the attempt to consider her situation rationally.

HENRIETTA: Wyoming. ... Of all places ...

SCENE EIGHT

Henrietta's Dream

Lights dim. HENRIETTA sits at her desk, leans back in her chair, closes her eyes and sleeps. A dance of lights creates a dream-world in which life, love and death are united. Dream music is heard. Enter KRYSTAL, dancing. A short while later, HARTHAUSER enters. He watches KRYSTAL, tries to emulate her, looks ridiculous, gives up. Each of them wears glasses with black frames and oddly shaped lenses. CROSSE enters. He also wears the odd glasses. He glances at a non-existent wrist watch, then addresses the audience.

CROSSE: Why do I consult a watch that isn't there? Lifetime habits die hard. Time governed my mortal life:

now time has no meaning. Therefore, I am not late. ... Where are we?

KRYSTAL: In a dream—Henrietta's dream.

HARTHAUSER: [Fusses with glasses] This way of seeing is hard to get used to. Are you sure it is her dream?

KRYSTAL: Yes.

HARTHAUSER: Where is she?

KRYSTAL: In her office at the *Gazette*.

HARTHAUSER: We are back in the offices of the *Gazette*! Are we running in circles?

CROSSE: We are in a parallel universe.

HARTHAUSER: What is a parallel universe?

CROSSE: It is a place that is here, not there.

HENRIETTA: I am glad you came. I have wanted to see you again.

CROSSE: I have wanted to see you.

KRYSTAL: So have I.

HARTHAUSER: Let's not get maudlin.

HENRIETTA: Are there hard feelings, Krystal?

KRYSTAL: No. No hard feelings. The heaviness is gone. I see now that Krystal Kracker lived a false life. Krystal is renewed in Katrina.

HENRIETTA: Katrina—your other self. I believe she has talent, but I was surprised that she is such a silly girl.

KRYSTAL: I love Katrina. She is enthusiastic about things. She is in love with life. Krystal was not.

HENRIETTA: Katrina is searching for love. Aren't we all? ... I wonder if Ben hired her.

KRYSTAL: She got the job. She is thrilled. I am glad that you gave her a chance.

HENRIETTA: How about you, Emil: can you forgive me?

HARTHAUSER: There is no need for forgiveness. I am beyond that.

HENRIETTA: Henry Hardstone is your replacement.

HARTHAUSER: He is a disappointment. I would as soon be replaced by a basset hound. Hardstone has no pride: pleading for mercy, willing to take a low-level job. I started in the executive suite.

CROSSE: Installed by your uncle.

HARTHAUSER: Uncle Ferdy, my Regent. In the Brahmin world I grew up in, inheritance was everything. It was not a good preparation for life. ... I had no happiness in my life. I didn't think it was important to be happy. Now I know differently.

HENRIETTA: You were married, you had children. Surely your family was a source of happiness.

HARTHAUSER: Emil Harthauser had no idea how to be happy. He married and had a family because that was what he was supposed to do. There was no joy in it, no love. He pursued other women, but there was no love in that either. ... He has traded an unsatisfactory life for that of a wanderer. He has yet to find that elusive thing called love.

HENRIETTA: What about you, Julian?

CROSSE: I had my way with women—until I met you, Henrietta. You pleaded with me. I played my usual game, not realizing that I was playing poker with Fate. The game was going my way: I had an excellent hand. Fate had four aces.

HARTHAUSER: More precisely, three bullets.

HENRIETTA: Did you have a wife, Julian?

CROSSE: I did. We would get together from time to time, even after we divorced.

HENRIETTA: Did you have children?

CROSSE: My wife had a boy and a girl. If the man who paid child support can be counted as the father, they were mine.

HENRIETTA: Jarret Thorne will replace you.

CROSSE: Beware, Henrietta. Jarret will snare you.

HENRIETTA: Don't be too sure of that. My life is not predictable. I like it that way—the feeling that anything might happen.

KRYSTAL: You don't have enough time to think that way, Henrietta. Think instead that something *must* happen, something good. Katrina is thinking that way. She will find love. She will have a better life than I did.

HARTHAUSER: If Hardstone has any of me in him, he will find his way. He might end up in my old job.

HENRIETTA: I like his chances. [**Addresses CROSSE**] Have you forgiven me, Julian?

CROSSE: I hold no grudges. I have one regret: that I did not get to know you, possibly to love you.

HENRIETTA: I have the same regret.

CROSSE: Our regrets will pass. The mountain is stead-fast; the wind—like our passions—blows hot and cold. Krystal has spoken wisely.

HENRIETTA: If something good is to happen, think of it as something that *must* happen. I see her point.... I am tired—very tired. ... I— I can't go on.

> At her desk, **HENRIETTA rests her head on folded arms.**

KRYSTAL: I miss sleep.

CROSSE: I miss vodka martinis.

HARTHAUSER: Are you sure Henrietta is asleep? It looks like a very deep sleep, perhaps her last.

KRYSTAL: She is between two worlds. It is dangerous.

CROSSE: You have learned a lot Krystal—more than I have. Perhaps you should be our leader.

KRYSTAL: You are best for the job, Crosse. Confucius says: better to follow an optimistic fool than a pessimistic one.

HARTHAUSER: I follow you, Crosse, because I have no idea what to do. ... Where are we going?

CROSSE: There is no such thing as where. Our destina-tion is not a place but a state of being: Nirvana.

HARTHAUSER: Are you sure, Crosse, that there really is a Nirvana?

> **CROSSE shrugs. Dream lights go down as the ghostly trio exits. HENRIETTA sleeps a deep sleep. A few mo-ments pass. The door opens, FREDDY enters.**

FREDDY: Oh no! [Runs to HENRIETTA's side] For God's sake, Henrietta, breathe!

FREDDY nudges her shoulder; she takes a deep breath and continues breathing and sleeping.

FREDDY: Thank goodness!

FREDDY takes HENRIETTA's jacket from the coat rack, places it over her shoulders, then exits quietly. A glowing light fades slowly to black.

FINI

Dreams

Tales of the Commedia dell'Arte

Part One

Harlequin: The Quest for Isabella

SCENE SUMMARY

One: at breakfast, the present
Two: a Nordic castle, 16th century
Three: Arugula, a town on the west coast of Italy, 16th century
Four: the Nordic castle, 16th century
Five: Arugula, 16th century
Six: A desolate beach, 16th Century
Seven-Ten: Arugula, 16th century
Eleven: at breakfast, the present

CHARACTERS [1]

Husband, a statistical wizard
Wife, a dreamer
Sieglinde, a Viking queen
Lorenzo, Duke of Arugula
Musician (non-speaking)
Servant (non-speaking)
Olaf, a Viking king
Captain Bravado, soldier, braggart
Harlequin, actor, adventurer
Cassandro, a lawyer
Gudrun, attendant to Queen Sieglinde
Voluptua, a seamstress
Flaminia, Captain Bravado's (unhappy) wife
Commander Erik, a Viking
Helga, attendant to Queen Sieglinde
Scapino, factotum, a hustler

---

[1] Note: With part doubling—making use of masks and simple costumes (capes, hats, glasses, beards, etc.)—all parts can be played by seven to nine performers. Scenes flow into each other, time is elastic.

Orsella, a fortune teller
Argeo, an astrologer
Colombina, purveyor of potions
Pantalone, Mayor of Arugula
Page (non-speaking)
Ottavio, a gentleman
Isabella, Duchess of Arugula

Scene One

HUSBAND and WIFE are at the breakfast table. Silence. The usual table routines: pouring coffee, buttering bread, etc. HUSBAND reads newspaper, WIFE daydreams.

HUSBAND: Pass the marmalade.

WIFE: I'll have a crumpet.

HUSBAND: Gooseberry or strawberry?

WIFE: Gooseberry! How unusual. I will have it.

HUSBAND passes a plate, WIFE takes the crumpet.

HUSBAND: Market is down ... Weather, more rain than sun ... What do you know: the high school hockey team has a chance at the state championship. Tim Tyler coaches that team.

WIFE: Uh-huh ... Might I have the Fashion Section.

HUSBAND passes a section of the newspaper to WIFE. They read quietly. Abruptly, HUSBAND sets down the newspaper and stares at WIFE, his expression suggesting that there is something about her that baffles him.

WIFE: [**Not taking her eyes off the newspaper**] Why are you staring? [**Faces HUSBAND**] Is there something wrong with me?

HUSBAND: You dreamed last night.

WIFE: I always dream.

HUSBAND: Last night's dream must have been very exciting.

WIFE: Oh—?

HUSBAND: You tossed, you turned, you laughed, you cried. What was it about?

WIFE: [Airily evasive] You know how it is with dreams: they vanish when you wake up.

HUSBAND: [Airily skeptical] I see.

WIFE: You never ask about my dreams.

HUSBAND: The reason I asked is that I, too, had a dream.

WIFE: How rare!

HUSBAND: You were in my dream.

WIFE: Even rarer! I have never heard you say that I was in one of your dreams.

HUSBAND: I never have said it.

WIFE: We've been married twenty-two years and this is—

HUSBAND: Be precise. [A mental computation] Twenty-two years, four months, three days and seventeen hours.

WIFE: I am not interested in precision. I am interested in the fact that, after twenty-two, four, three and seventeen, this is the first time that I have been in one of your dreams.

HUSBAND: It is odd, isn't it? But then I hardly ever dream. My first dream—since we married—occurred the night after our fifth anniversary. Since then I have had—[**A quick calculation**]—exactly sixteen dreams.

WIFE: I dream almost every night.

HUSBAND: I know. You are so restless. [**Intensely curious**] How many of your dreams am I in?

WIFE: I haven't kept count.

HUSBAND: Was I in last night's dream?

WIFE: You were.

HUSBAND: What was I doing?

WIFE: The first question you should ask is who you were.

HUSBAND: I was someone else?

WIFE: In my life, you are husband: statistical wizard, successful businessman—one of the world's masters. In my dreams you are a burglar—sometimes a magician—a man of many guises. Last night you were the Thief of Hearts. You wore a mask.

HUSBAND: A mask!

WIFE: It was part of your character.

HUSBAND: What was the masked man doing?

WIFE: I will tell you, but first I want to know what I was doing in your dream.

HUSBAND: It was centuries ago. You lived in a castle. The scene was saturated in moonlight. You wore an ivory gown decorated with pearls.

WIFE: [Shaken] How odd—how very odd this is.

HUSBAND: Oh—?

WIFE: In my dream I lived in a castle. It was a bright moonlit night. I wore a pearl-studded ivory gown.

HUSBAND: And a mask—

WIFE: I did not wear a mask.

HUSBAND: The lady in my dream did. Her name was Isabella.

WIFE: I don't know what my name was. My masked suitor addressed me as "beloved," "my treasure," and, as his passion grew, "regal desire of my heart."

HUSBAND: Regal desire of my heart! I can't imagine myself saying that.

WIFE: In the sixteenth century you would. You wore a shirt of many colors and tight pants—very tight.

HUSBAND: Did this masked man in tight pants seduce you?

WIFE: He tried to.

HUSBAND: What happened?

WIFE: Before he could succeed, I woke up. ... In your dream did you try to seduce Isabella?

HUSBAND: I was a man with a mission: to rescue Isabella from her castle-prison.

WIFE: What happened?

HUSBAND: I suddenly realized that Isabella was you. I woke up.

WIFE: Do you suppose it was a shared dream?

HUSBAND: That is unheard of.

WIFE: Until now.

HUSBAND: It wasn't a shared dream: the details are different. In your dream, I wore a mask. In my dream, you were masked.

WIFE: I did not wear a mask—I am sure of it.

HUSBAND: And I am equally certain that I—[**Pause, reflects**] Do you suppose that we deceive ourselves?

WIFE: I see what you mean: we see the masks that others present to the world, but not our own.

HUSBAND: Let's suppose that we did wear masks. What was mine like?

WIFE: It was black trimmed with gold; high cheekbones, laughing eyes.

HUSBAND: Handsome—a little roguish, I suppose.

WIFE: Handsome indeed, except for the nose: it resembled an eagle's beak.

HUSBAND: A sign of mathematical and statistical genius—and, I suppose, business acumen.

WIFE: I can think of other interpretations. But let's not dwell on that: I am eager to know what my mask was like.

HUSBAND: It was elegant—as white as the full moon that illuminated the scene. It was decorated with jewels; there were touches of vermillion about the edges; the cheeks were pink, the nose, petite.

WIFE: Ah! An elegant woman.

HUSBAND: The only flaw was the mouth. There was a bit of drooling at the lower edge.

WIFE: [Appalled] Drooling!

HUSBAND: Most likely it was brought on by those tight pants.

HUSBAND and WIFE are absorbed in thought.

WIFE: I have a feeling that we are we still dreaming.

HUSBAND: We are having breakfast.

More thinking, mind reading.

WIFE: A waking dream. For example, I see an image in your head—what is it?

HUSBAND: A room with stone walls. I suppose it is in a castle. [Puzzled] What is that kaleidoscopic image in your head?

WIFE: It is a town square. There is a story to be told. It will play out in the castle and the town square. Deep secrets are revealed in dreams. A centuries-old story affects us.

HUSBAND: What sort of story?

WIFE: We will find out. I can't wait for the next dream. It will be interesting to meet people who lived five-hundred years ago.

HUSBAND: At least they won't be people we know.

WIFE: Are you afraid that your mistress will show up?

HUSBAND: There is no mistress!

WIFE: If that woman has the audacity to show up in one of my dreams, I will resort to murder.

WIFE picks up table knife and points it at HUSBAND.

HUSBAND: I would prefer poison. The idea of a sharp object penetrating my hide horrifies me.

WIFE: [**Again wielding the knife**] If she appears—no matter how disguised—I will recognize her.

HUSBAND: You frighten me. Perhaps we should abandon this project.

WIFE: We have gone too far. I am committed to it.

HUSBAND: There is a danger—

WIFE: Our settled lives could be turned downside-up.

HUSBAND: Not to mention outside-in.

WIFE: After twenty-two yawning years, four boring months and three dull days, it is time to live dangerously.

HUSBAND: Very well. We begin tonight.

Silence. WIFE turns to breakfast table. HUSBAND is distraught.

WIFE: Your head is filled with white granules. What is it you want—salt or sugar?

HUSBAND: The white granules are snowflakes.

WIFE: Snowflakes! At this time of year?

HUSBAND: [**Panicky**] The inside of my head is a refrigerator.

WIFE: We both see the snowflakes. We are still dreaming! How can we break out of it?

HUSBAND: [**Shivering**] I don't know. A cold brain can't think. Do something— anything—quickly!

WIFE: Something, anything—what? Oh, I know.

WIFE pinches HUSBAND's nose.

HUSBAND: Ouch! That hurt!

WIFE: The snowflakes are gone.

HUSBAND: Thank goodness! 11,304 of them.

WIFE: The dream is over. I've lost it already.

HUSBAND: It is good to be back to normal.

WIFE: The routine is comforting.

HUSBAND butters a piece of toast. WIFE pours coffee.

HUSBAND: Pass the marmalade.

WIFE: I'll have a crumpet.

HUSBAND: Gooseberry or strawberry ...

WIFE: Gooseberry! How unusual. I will have it.

HUSBAND: [**Puzzled**] Oh! You already have a gooseberry tart.

WIFE: [**Perplexed**] That's odd. I have no recollection of taking it. ... Do you suppose I was dreaming—a waking dream?

HUSBAND shrugs, returns to newspaper, WIFE nibbles tart.

HUSBAND: Market is down ... Weather, more rain than sun ... What do you know: the high school hockey team has a chance at the state championship. Tim Tyler coaches that team.

WIFE: Uh-huh ... Might I have the Fashion Section.

HUSBAND flips through newspaper.

HUSBAND: This is odd. I don't see it.

WIFE sees the Fashion Section on the floor next to her chair.

WIFE: I already have it.

HUSBAND: How do you suppose that happened?

WIFE shrugs, reads paper. HUSBAND tries to puzzle it out.

FADE TO BLACK

Scene Two

A Nordic castle. LORENZO is closing in on SIEGLINDE. HUSBAND and WIFE are asleep.

SIEGLINDE: Lorenzo, would you please instruct your greedy eyes to stop devouring me.

LORENZO: I would do that, your majesty, if only you would command yourself to be less fascinating.

SIEGLINDE: A queen commands others, not herself. Besides, it is her duty to be fascinating.

LORENZO: Then why should I not be fascinated?

SIEGLINDE: I expect you to be fascinated—but with self-control. No ogling. The servants will notice it, and they do gossip.

LORENZO: I have dismissed the servants.

SIEGLINDE: Olaf might enter at any moment.

LORENZO: He won't mind my being here: I am his guest, just as he was my guest in Arugula.

SIEGLINDE: Discretion, Lorenzo, discretion! If Olaf were to catch you ogling you would find out what a Viking rage is like.

LORENZO: Dear Sieglinde, you worry excessively. Your husband—your Olaf, and that bunch of Viking rowdies he calls his knights—seated themselves about the round table four hours ago. They demolished a stag and drank three kegs of ale. Intoxicated by ale and a roaring fire they told tales of conquest and dragons slain; then, eyes-drooping as the great fire faded, they told dirty jokes—old ones. At last they fell asleep and will sleep the night through—all but one, yours truly—who slipped silently away to a secret rendezvous. Shall we to bed, my dear?

SIEGLINDE: You sound like Olaf—always in a hurry. He makes love the Viking way: bam-bam—doesn't even say thank you ma'am, then— [A snore]

LORENZO: I am sorry, my treasure, if I seemed impetuous. Do you really think that I, Lorenzo, who wears the cloak and cap of Arugula, would make love crudely? No, no, we will have music, wine and cakes. Then, as the romantic feeling blossoms, there will be soft kisses, tender embraces, and finally, ecstasy!

SIEGLINDE: Oh, Lorenzo, I am ready for ecstasy! I will follow you, but you must be guided by me. Now, cool your passion a few moments while I prepare myself for romance.

> SIEGLINDE closes her eyes and meditates. Not fully awake, HUSBAND enters the dream.

HUSBAND: Time out. I am trying to figure this out. A Viking king named Olaf is married to a spoiled girl named Sieglinde, who does not love him, though he is in love with her.

WIFE: How do you know that?

HUSBAND: Bam-bam—he is trying.

WIFE: All he wants from her is a son—an heir. Try to understand Sieglinde's view: she wants romance in her life.

HUSBAND: So she yields to a lover, Lorenzo, Duke of Arugula, not realizing that Lorenzo and Olaf are flip sides of one coin.

WIFE: If Sieglinde is clever, she will keep the coin from flipping over. I want to see how it works out. Dream on.

HUSBAND and WIFE resume sleeping.

SIEGLINDE: I am ready, Lorenzo. Be gallant, be gentle.

LORENZO: My beloved, allow me, your humble servant, to prepare for you a joyous evening.

MUSICIAN enters and plays. LORENZO and SIEGLINDE dance. An awkward, but enthusiastic dancer, SIEGLINDE feels free in the movement of the dance.

SIEGLINDE: The music is sublime.

LORENZO: Sieglinde, my darling, you dance like an angel.

SIEGLINDE: The dance liberates the body, music, the spirit.

LORENZO: That is the prelude to ecstasy.

As they dance, Duke's SERVANT enters and sets up a small table with wine and hors d'oeuvres, then exits. Music ends. MUSICIAN exits.

LORENZO: Come my dear, let me introduce you to a few of my chef's creations.

Sieglinde eats a confection, then another, then another

SIEGLINDE: How delectable! ... This is divine. ... This melts on the tongue. We Vikings have nothing as exquisite as this.

LORENZO: My chef is French, so is my wine master. He makes a wonderful cordial from strawberries

LORENZO pours the cordial. SIEGLINDE swallows it.

SIEGLINDE: How sweet! How delightfully sweet. This must be the nectar of the gods.

LORENZO refills SIEGLINDE'S glass. The cordial goes down easily.

SIEGLINDE: This is so sophisticated. I— ... Oh! It must be strong ... I am feeling giddy ...

LORENZO: The mood grows. Bliss awaits us.

SIEGLINDE: Oh, Lorenzo ...

LORENZO lavishes kisses upon SIEGLINDE. She is melting in his arms.

LORENZO: Come my dear, join me in a night of ecstasy.

SIEGLINDE: Yes, dearest Lorenzo ... ex ...stasy ... night ... of ... Oh, my head is spinning ...

LORENZO: Rest your precious head on my shoulder.

SIEGLINDE rests her head on LORENZO'S shoulder. He leads her toward an off-stage bedroom. After a few wobbly steps, SIEGLINDE collapses in his arms.

LORENZO: She is out cold! Rotten luck! The wine was too much for her. **[Sets the sleeping SIEGLINDE in a chair.]** I thought Vikings could handle their liquor.

LORENZO removes his cloak and cap and tosses them to SERVANT.

LORENZO: She is all yours, Olaf.

In a light that suggests a wheel rotating on the stage floor, the actor slowly rotates, SERVANT dresses him in a Viking helmet and leather vest. He is now OLAF, a rough-hewn, blunt-spoken Viking. He studies the Queen sympathetically.

OLAF: Half a pint of ale and she is out. Olaf learned that a long time ago.

OLAF tosses SIEGLINDE over his shoulder, takes two steps then addresses audience.

OLAF: It's the Viking way.

OLAF walks off, carrying SIEGLINDE. WIFE and HUSBAND awaken.

WIFE: Lorenzo turned out to be a fool. There is no need to romance a woman with a dessert wine that goes down like juice and is loaded with alcohol. A duke ought to know that.

HUSBAND: Dukes do know it. That is how they get to be dukes. Shall we have breakfast?

SCENE THREE

Arugula, a town in Italy, mid-sixteenth century. A mimed show in which characters come and go, gossiping, playing games, etc. All this activity is interrupted by the clatter of clashing swords heard off-stage.

Everyone scatters. Enter HARLEQUIN and CAPTAIN BRAVADO in a sword fight. HARLEQUIN'S sword flies from his hand. BRAVADO is poised to run him through.

BRAVADO: Prepare to die!

HARLEQUIN raises a hand: a stop sign.

HARLEQUIN: Stop!

BRAVADO: Do you expect me to stop at the moment my honor is to be vindicated?

HARLEQUIN: The idea of a sharp object penetrating my hide horrifies me. I would prefer poison.

BRAVADO: Poison! A woman's weapon! If you are to die, die like a man.

HARLEQUIN: Frankly, I would prefer to live like a man.

BRAVADO: My anger is justified. I caught you in my wife's arms. I must have satisfaction.

HARLEQUIN: You ought to tend to your own fireplace, Signore—I didn't get your name.

BRAVADO: I suppose a man is entitled to know who dispatched him. I am Captain Bravado, hero of Constantinople, defender of Arugula, feared by Vikings and Turks alike. I do not take insults lightly, and I apprehend that your remark—tend to your fireplace—is insulting.

HARLEQUIN: What it means is: if your wife falls into another man's embrace—fifteen minutes after he has arrived in town—you have been a negligent lover. Why should another man pay with his life for your lack of honor in love?

BRAVADO: You have added insult to injury. You have questioned my virility. I, Bravado, who has sprinkled the known world with lively offspring. Prepare to die!

A sword thrust. Harlequin deftly eludes it.

HARLEQUIN: Be cautious! Do you see that ring? It was placed on my finger by the Doge of Venice, when he assigned me my mission. The man who stops my life before that mission is accomplished will die a horrible death and he will spend eternity in hell.

Intimidated, BRAVADO makes the Sign of the Cross.

BRAVADO: What is this mission?

HARLEQUIN: It is to find and rescue Isabella.

BRAVADO: There are lots of Isabellas.

HARLEQUIN: There is only one divine Isabella— Isabella divina. I have spent three years searching for her.

BRAVADO: [Astonished] Three years?

HARLEQUIN: I have traveled all over this boot-shaped peninsula; I have performed for three commedia companies. I have entertained a thousand audiences. Through all that I have never lost sight of my mission: to find Isabella and set her free.

BRAVADO: Amazing! You probably don't realize it, but you have finally arrived at the right place. After three years of wandering you are moments away from seeing this legendary woman, and you will die by my sword before you get to see her. What a tragedy! My story—and yours—will be told by poets for a thousand years. Prepare to die.

Another sword thrust. HARLEQUIN evades it.

HARLEQUIN: Just a minute. Who is this dream of poets I am to die for?

BRAVADO: Isabella, wife of Duke Lorenzo, who holds her prisoner in his castle. His marriage is loveless, yet he is the most jealous of men. His weapon of choice is a canon. He loves to blow huge holes in—

HARLEQUIN: Stop! I can't stand the thought of a huge hole where my chest once was.

BRAVADO: The sword is preferable. Stand still and take the steel like a man.

HARLEQUIN: I must see Isabella before I die.

BRAVADO: It is impossible. Your time is up. There can be no further delay.

Another sword thrust, again evaded by Harlequin.

HARLEQUIN: [**Calls out**] Is there anyone in this wretched town who might help me?

Enter CASSANDRO

CASSANDRO: I am Cassandro, counselor at law. Do you wish me to represent you?

HARLEQUIN: Yes.

BRAVADO: You will have to represent his corpse.

CASSANDRO: Has he offended you?

BRAVADO: I caught him with my wife in his arms.

CASSANDRO: My dear Bravado, you must make allowance for the fact that he is a stranger in town. If you must defend your honor, challenge the men in town who have embraced your Flaminia. You will have more duels than you can handle.

BRAVADO: [**Points sword at CASSANDRO**] You have questioned my wife's integrity. Prepare to defend yourself.

CASSANDRO: I carry no sword. As a lawyer, I am exempted from section 501(c)(3) of the chivalric code: the use of a weapon to defend one's honor. I defend my honor with fees. [**Points a finger at Bravado**] Insult me, and my fee doubles.

Exit BRAVADO, frustrated, indignant.

HARLEQUIN: Thank you for answering my appeal, Signore Cassandro. I am Harlequin. I also answer to Harley, a name given to me affectionately by my many admirers.

CASSANDRO: What is your problem?

HARLEQUIN: This Bravado is my problem. If I encounter him anywhere, he will want to run me through.

CASSANDRO: When next you meet him, accept the challenge. Take the sword, swish it about so that it seems to cut the very air; then snarl, growl, fight like a game-cock—and watch him run. He brags incessantly about his military achievements. Give him a glass of wine and he will leap on to a table and tell you how he led the charge that routed the Turks at Constantinople. Upon encountering a Turk with a scimitar, Bravado set a speed record in retreat. The Turk collapsed in a fit of laughter. Since the Turk was on the ground, Bravado counts it as a victory. He is all bluff and bluster, but is in fact a coward.

HARLEQUIN: Thanks for the advice. I no longer fear him.

CASSANDRO: My advice is not free.

HARLEQUIN removes a coin from his purse and drops it into CASSANDRO's purse.

CASSANDRO: What brings you to Arugula?

HARLEQUIN: I have come to rescue Isabella.

CASSANDRO: Ah, my friend, I advise you to leave town immediately. Your quest is hopeless; and, when Duke Lorenzo finds out about you, it will cost you your life.

HARLEQUIN: I have an idea—an inspiration: let's not tell the Duke.

CASSANDRO: He will find out. He has spies everywhere.

HARLEQUIN: Perhaps—

CASSANDRO: No point in discussing it. In addition to being a lawyer, I am a magistrate. My request that you leave Arugula is now an order. It is in your own best interest. Go now, go quickly.

> **Despondent, HARLEQUIN exits. CASSANDRO gazes in the direction of the castle.**

CASSANDRO: Isabella, most noble of women, devoted to true love not marriages arranged for power or fortune. You loved my nephew, Ottavio, but you could not have him. Your father thought that my family name was too low to be associated with his exalted name. That man, who does not deserve to be called a father, feels no remorse for the suffering he has inflicted upon his daughter. Poor Isabella! All mankind weeps for you, but none can save you. Only poets will redeem you. You will live in their works as the symbol of fidelity and unrequited love.

> **CASSANDRO sighs, exits. WIFE and HUSBAND appear.**

WIFE: Unrequited love! No woman wants to be a statue in a glass case. We haven't even gotten to see Isabella.

HUSBAND: I like the way Harley got out of that duel.

WIFE: Why is it that you, who rarely dream, have met your alter-ego, Harlequin, and I, the romantic dreamer, cannot meet Isabella?

HUSBAND: [**A calculation**] There are 256 possible answers to that question.

WIFE: Thanks.

HUSBAND: Shall we have breakfast?

SCENE FOUR

The Viking castle. OLAF is studying a map. GUDRUN enters.

GUDRUN: Good morning, your majesty.

OLAF: Good morning, Gudrun. Where is your mistress?

GUDRUN: It is my unhappy duty to report that Queen Sieglinde has fled.

OLAF closes his eyes and reflects a few moments.

OLAF: It doesn't surprise me. She has been awfully secretive these past few days. ... Where is she going?

GUDRUN: Her destination is a secret, but I have found it out: Italy.

OLAF: Italy! That is a hazardous undertaking, especially for a pregnant woman.

GUDRUN: She believes that the Italian sun and mineral baths will result in a healthy child.

OLAF: Who is accompanying the Queen?

GUDRUN: Helga—the most trusted of her ladies-in-waiting.

OLAF: Who gave you this information?

GUDRUN: Helga. I wheedled it out of her. The girl is loyal but simple.

OLAF: Where in Italy are they going?

GUDRUN: To Duke Lorenzo's town: Arugula.

OLAF: [Astonished, upset] Would she still want to see Lorenzo?

GUDRUN: When he visited us he very much admired the Queen.

OLAF: As a lover, he was a bust.

GUDRUN: The Queen blames herself for the failure of that romance.

OLAF: Can she possibly believe that? How do you know it?

GUDRUN: Helga. The Queen also believes that Lorenzo is not married.

OLAF: He has a wife—Isabella. It is an unhappy marriage, but Lorenzo won't let her go. [Reminiscing] We attacked Arugula—three years ago. Lorenzo surrendered without a fight and invited us to have a vacation in sunny Italy. It was a great morale booster for the troops.

GUDRUN: Commander Erik, my husband, still talks of the music, sunshine, good food—*la dolce vita* he calls it.

OLAF: I am told that when the men recall it they drink a toast to good King Olaf.

GUDRUN: They do.

OLAF: I could send a fast vessel to overtake her. ... On the other hand, maybe the Queen ought to have her way. Experience of the world would do her good. ... Besides, I would welcome an Italian vacation myself. [**To GUDRUN**] Give a message to Commander Erik. I want a ship and crew made ready.

GUDRUN bows and exits. OLAF studies the map a few moments, then exits. HUSBAND and WIFE appear.

HUSBAND: The plot seems to be thickening.

WIFE: I am not sure I like it.

HUSBAND: It might be exciting. Maybe in the next dream we'll get to sail on a Viking ship.

WIFE: That is not for me. They didn't have Dramamine in those days.

HUSBAND: Shall we have breakfast?

SCENE FIVE

Arugula. VOLUPTUA and FLAMINIA enter.

VOLUPTUA: Inside every civilized man is a brute. They show you such a pretty veneer, but once they get past a girl's petticoat the brute comes out.

FLAMINIA: Your problem, Voluptua, is that you fail to control the situation.

VOLUPTUA: My dear Flaminia, you are not one to talk about controlling the situation. Men about town boast that with you they always hit the jackpot.

FLAMINIA: They are windbags, just like the windbag my father forced me to marry—Captain Bravado, who treats me like a slave and gives me barely enough money to maintain the household. There is no money for dresses, yet I am well dressed; I have rings and earrings and pretty bracelets. Men find me attractive: they lavish gifts on me. And they never hit the jackpot—well, almost never. One gets a headache; sometimes there is an interruption (arranged by me): "My husband is nearby," or: "Is that your wife who is approaching?" A wife, tipped off, will always show up.

VOLUPTUA: I wish I could copy your style, Flaminia, but I can't. All I want is a man who will be a real lover.

FLAMINIA: I am tired of being Missis Bravado. Oh, Voluptua, keep it a secret, but I may have found Mister Right. I was getting to know him when my husband discovered us.

VOLUPTUA: Is he the fellow called Harley, who made a fool of your husband?

FLAMINIA: How did you know about him?

VOLUPTUA: Every woman in town is talking about him.

FLAMINIA: Oh my! I underestimated the speed of women's tongues. ... Well, let them talk: Harley is mine.

VOLUPTUA: Control your passion, Flaminia. Harley will disappoint you. The perfect man does not exist.

FLAMINIA: I don't expect perfection: I would take my chances with Harley. Men have all sorts of passions: fat passions, skinny passions, pointy-nose passions, bulb-nose passions. Some remind me of birds: the overweight owl, who—ready to swoop on his tender little prey—falls from the tree. Then there is the parakeet: "Hey-ho cutie, how'dya like the rainbow on my back." ... Harley's is an eagle's passion: a firm brow, cruel, yet tender.

VOLUPTUA: He sounds intriguing.

FLAMINIA: He is not the man for you, Voluptua. You are a seamstress: marry a tailor.

VOLUPTUA: There are five tailors in town: all are taken.

FLAMINIA: Burattino, the innkeeper, recently lost his wife.

VOLUPTUA: Fatso—as he is known—spends his money on his serving girls. His wife died half starved, in rags, and bored. Fatso is not for me.

FLAMINIA: Serafino, the church sexton is available; so is Butto, the shoemaker.

VOLUPTUA: One is saturated with incense, the other is made up of patches of leather, stitched together. I will marry when I find the man who is right for me.

FLAMINIA: If you wait too long, your father will decide for you. And you know what kind of man a father thinks is right for his daughter—

Taking turns, one mimes the action, the other describes it, accompanied by laughter.

FLAMINIA/VOLUPTUA:—grouchy ... suspicious ... stingy ... past his prime—[**In unison**] and a heavy load to bear.

A great racket is heard without.

VOLUPTUA: Good heavens! Are we at war?

Enter HARLEQUIN and BRAVADO engaged in a duel with swords. HARLEQUIN's attack is vigorous. BRAVADO's sword flies out of his hand.

HARLEQUIN: Prepare to die!

BRAVADO: Have mercy, Sir Harlequin.

HARLEQUIN: You issued the challenge. You said that this time my life would not be spared. Why should I spare yours?

BRAVADO: There is Flaminia—my beautiful wife. Would you kill a man in the presence of his wife?

Both men look to FLAMINIA.

FLAMINIA: I'll leave.

BRAVADO: Have mercy on me, Flaminia.

FLAMINIA exits, beckoning VOLUPTUA to follow her. VOLUPTUA starts to follow, but lingers.

VOLUPTUA: Are you Harley?

Mesmerized by VOLUPTUA, HARLEQUIN forgets BRAVADO.

HARLEQUIN: Yes, dream of my life, I am Harley. What an enchanting creature you are. Such a beauty can only be Isabella.

BRAVADO sneaks off.

VOLUPTUA: I am Isabella.

HARLEQUIN: At last I have found you.

VOLUPTUA: [**Aside**] I'll have my name changed.

HARLEQUIN: I have been sent by Heaven to free you.

VOLUPTUA: I thank Heaven for sending you! ... Whoever you are ...

HARLEQUIN: I am Harlequin. I come from the North—that is to say the southeastern part of the mid-western North. I am an actor, a jester, an acrobat, a musician, a desperado—a man who will throw everything over to have the woman he truly loves.

VOLUPTUA: Your words have won my heart.

HARLEQUIN: Will you marry me, Isabella?

VOLUPTUA: My dearest, yes, yes, yes. Come with me. I know of a secret place where no one will disturb us.

HARLEQUIN: Are you sure we won't be disturbed? I have traveled the length and breadth of this boot-shaped peninsula and have yet to find a genuinely safe hiding place. Everywhere you go there are gossips, snoops, spies, vagabonds, bandits, process servers, constables—not to mention lovers and other lunatics.

VOLUPTUA: Friar Laurence will hide us. He is the patron saint of desperate lovers. He has marvelous potions, and he is empowered to perform all rites and rituals. He can change names—first and last; he can change my name to yours.

HARLEQUIN: I will caress you, Isabella. My lips will kiss your luscious lips. I will venture south to savor delicious melons; thence to the hot equator—

VOLUPTUA yanks him off.

HARLEQUIN: —and I will go with you to Friar Laurence.

VOLUPTUA and HARLEQUIN run off. A few moments pass. Enter FLAMINIA.

FLAMINIA: Oh, no! Everything has gone awry! Harley and Voluptua are gone ... and Bravado's corpse is nowhere to be seen. ... Voluptua must have distracted Harley. ... I was foolish to leave him alone with her. Vamp! I thought she was a friend. Tramp! ... Where would she go? She has a secret hideaway—I know that—but she has kept it secret. ... Where might it be? ... I'll scour town and countryside to keep my Harley.

FLAMINIA exits. HUSBAND and WIFE appear.

WIFE: This is a peculiar development. Do you suppose they will marry?

HUSBAND: Who?

WIFE: Harley and Voluptua.

HUSBAND: Nothing will come of it. In the world of dreams, characters get things done only while they are on stage. Nothing gets done off-stage.

WIFE: Harley is lucky. Being off-stage saves him from his folly: having a friar named Laurence marry him to a chick named Voluptua, who he thinks is Isabella.

HUSBAND: Everything ends in confusion. This dream world can be frustrating!

WIFE: Shall we have breakfast?

SCENE SIX

A beach. KING OLAF and COMMANDER ERIK enter.

OLAF: A desolate beach. ... But it will do for a rest.

ERIK: The crew welcomes the break.

OLAF: You know, Erik, there was a time when everything was clear-cut. We knew what was right and wrong; we knew proper behavior. A woman who deserts her husband, be she a queen or a farmer's wife, was condemned by all.

ERIK: That is still the case. Nothing has changed.

OLAF: Things are changing. I sense it. A nagging doubt creeps in. Is it all her fault? Has the husband been negligent?

ERIK: We cannot be perfect, your Majesty. Nor can our wives be perfect. That is why we must insist on loyalty.

OLAF: But greater loyalty from our women.

ERIK: That is women's advantage. We men welcome the hunt and risk our lives in battle. It is our way of evening the score.

OLAF: My wife is not merely unhappy. She believes that another man is better than me.

ERIK: Perhaps, sir, a melancholy humor has got hold of her.

OLAF: I deal with domestic problems as my father did: by flying into a rage. Everyone in the castle trembles.

ERIK: Fear and trembling: it is the only proven system.

OLAF: For me—now—there is no proven system. Some invisible thing has defeated me. I believe it is called love. That girl—who I took sight unseen as part of a political deal—has managed to capture my heart.

ERIK: I have felt love myself, sir. Very impractical. Complicates things. Friendship is best.

OLAF: I pursue my wife knowing that I will catch up with her. When I do, I will find myself not victorious, but defeated. I will accept Sieglinde's decision.

ERIK: Might I suggest that we get back to the ship, sir. We have just enough daylight to reach our next port.

EXEUNT

SCENE SEVEN

Arugula. Enter SIEGLINDE, accompanied by HELGA.

SIEGLINDE: So this is Arugula. What a charming place. Little did Olaf imagine that his wife would one day enjoy *la dolce vita*. ... But our identities must remain secret. [**To HELGA**] What is your name?

HELGA is puzzled at being asked such an obvious question.

HELGA: Helga.

SIEGLINDE: Have you already forgotten—?

HELGA: Oh! My disguise name. It is Dina.

SIEGLINDE: And what is my name?

HELGA: Queen Sieglinde.

SIEGLINDE rolls her eyes.

HELGA: Oh, your disguise name. It is Lady Dolitta— no, that's not right. It is Lady Do- Do- Dorinda. Lady Dorinda.

Enter SCAPINO

SCAPINO: Good morning ladies. Welcome to Arugula. I am Scapino, at your service.

SIEGLINDE: What service do you perform?

SCAPINO: I do all sorts of things. I tell tales, realistic and fabulous. I play the flute and the mandolin. I sing songs: merry, sad, satirical. I entertain at weddings. I am a mood-maker at funerals: my sad face and melancholy songs make mourners weep; my happy face and satirical songs make them laugh.

SIEGLINDE: I have never heard of laughing mourners. Do you have merry funerals in Arugula?

SCAPINO: It depends on who has died. When Padre Bartolomeo, a poor priest, died, my melancholy songs had his mourners sobbing and sighing. There was a priest, Avariccio, who grew rich and fat, who abused his servants, whose sermons and prayers were uninspired. At his funeral my bawdy songs had his mourners roaring with laughter.

SIEGLINDE: What else do you do?

SCAPINO: I arrange marriages and other amorous adventures; I am a prophet, a magician—and a travel agent. How may I serve you?

SIEGLINDE: The castle on the hill—I suppose that is Duke Lorenzo's residence.

SCAPINO: It is. Between us, the Duke's mother, Lidia, runs the place. The Duke is too busy with his concubines to pay much attention to the affairs of state. To his credit, however, he had one stroke of diplomatic genius—Machiavelli praised him for it. When the Vikings attacked he personally met King Olaf and persuaded him and his men to take a vacation.

SIEGLINDE: I have heard that story. ... Who is the woman pacing on the castle rampart?

SCAPINO: That is the Duchess, Isabella. Hers is a sad story. She fell in love with a man beneath her station. Her father was furious and forced her to marry a man who was not her choice: Duke Lorenzo. She is his prisoner until she yields to him. She has refused to do it. To occupy her time, she drills the army.

SIEGLINDE: Concubines! A wife! An unhappy wife whose only recreation is to drill the army ... I had thought to visit Lorenzo, but now I am not sure I want to. ... Tell me, Signore Scapino, who is Isabella's true love—the man her father rejected?

SCAPINO: His name is Ottavio. He is of a good family, but not upper crust.

SIEGLINDE: Is Ottavio married?

SCAPINO: No. He lives with his mother.

SIEGLINDE: I'd like you to take me on a tour of the town. I want to see all the sights. ... And I would like to meet Ottavio. Can you arrange it?

SCAPINO: It will be expensive. I will have to bribe Oratio, the gate keeper ... Pasquea, Mama's nurse ... Laetitia, the housekeeper, who watches everything ...

Upon mention of each bribe to be paid, SIEGLINDE drops another coin into SCAPINO'S extended purse.

SCAPINO: I believe I can manage it. ... Who shall I introduce to Ottavio?

SIEGLINDE: The Lady Dorinda, Princess of Poland, presently residing in Parma. Come Dina.

Perplexed, HELGA looks about for Dina.

SIEGLINDE: Dina, wake up.

HELGA: Dina? Oh, that's me.

SCAPINO leads the ladies away.

SCENE EIGHT

HARLEQUIN enters. He stares in the direction of the castle.

HARLEQUIN: I have been ordered to leave town but—though it cost me my life—I cannot bring myself to do it. That image—Isabella, pacing on the rampart—consumes my soul. What has become of me—a jester who took nothing but his art seriously? ... What will happen to me? If only a man could know what the future will bring.

The word "future" is heard as a series of echoes.

ORSELLA: I hear the voice of one who seeks to know his future. I am Orsella, psychic, visionary. If you wish to consult me you must provide inspiration.

HARLEQUIN puts a coin into ORSELLA'S extended hand.

ORSELLA: Let me see your left hand. Very positive! The strong line that traverses your palm tells me that you are destined to find your true love. Next, the right hand. Oh, confusion! The strong line is crossed in two places; and there are so many weak lines. Your true love is beyond your grasp.

HARLEQUIN: I have found my true love; she is beyond my grasp. That is the present, not the future. You have told me nothing I don't already know.

ORSELLA: In your case, the present is the future.

HARLEQUIN: That is nonsense! I demand a refund.

ORSELLA: If you want a refund you have to return the commodity you received.

HARLEQUIN: What I received were words. How does one return words?

ORSELLA hands HARLEQUIN a box with a lid.

ORSELLA: This is our returns box.

HARLEQUIN opens lid and speaks into the box.

HARLEQUIN: Left hand, positive. You will find your true love. Right hand, confusion. Your true love is beyond your grasp. In your case, the present is the future.

HARLEQUIN clamps lid on box, hands it to ORSELLA and extends his hand for a refund.

ORSELLA: Just a moment.

ORSELLA opens the lid. Gibberish flies out.

ORSELLA: You have returned damaged goods. No refund.

ORSELLA scoots off. ARGEO enters.

ARGEO: Your mistake, Signore Harlequin, was to trust a fortune teller. They make a hundred guesses in a day. If one turns out to be right, they advertise it everywhere, forgetting the ninety-nine failures. The gullible are forever deceived. My approach is objective: I do not give you an opinion, I discover secrets that the heavens hold. **[Produces diplomas and certificates]** I am Argeo, doctor of astrology, University of Bologna. I am a charter member of the Geocosmic Society, the Rosicrucian Fellowship, etcetera, etcetera.

HARLEQUIN: The heavens are vast and distant. How do you figure out what secrets they hold?

ARGEO: I will answer the question upon due consideration.

HARLEQUIN drops a coin into ARGEO'S extended hand, ARGEO looks about to be sure no one is listening, lowers voice.

ARGEO: Your passion is for the Lady Isabella.

HARLEQUIN: How do you know that?

ARGEO: [**A gesture toward the heavens**] It just comes to me. Now, to continue, I have already determined the Lady Isabella's heavenly influences. Venus is her guiding star.

HARLEQUIN: There are some who say that Venus is a planet.

ARGEO: Star or planet, Venus is the most brilliant presence in the sky. As a heavenly influence it is prized by all who can afford it.

HARLEQUIN: How did you determine that Venus is Isabella's heavenly influence?

ARGEO: When she heard of my fame, she summoned me to the castle to help her see her future.

HARLEQUIN: If you saw her future, my question is simple: was I in it?

ARGEO: [**Again, lowers his voice**] A man was in it, but his identity was not revealed. Was it you or another man? We shall find out.

ARGEO extends his hand for another coin.

HARLEQUIN: I paid you.

ARGEO: You require lots of explanation. Your down payment has been exhausted.

The coin HARLEQUIN drops into ARGEO'S hand is obviously of lesser value. ARGEO bites it. HARLEQUIN flexes his muscles.

ARGEO: A person's character—and destiny—is influenced by the zodiac sign that is rising on the eastern horizon at the moment of his birth. Where were you born?

HARLEQUIN: Bergamo.

ARGEO unrolls a chart and studies it.

ARGEO: Ah! I have located the celestial sector in which Bergamo lies. What is the date of your birth?

HARLEQUIN: I was born on the sixth day of the month.

ARGEO: At what hour?

HARLEQUIN: My mother told me that my birth ruined her night's sleep, which is to say I was born in the wee hours of the morning.

ARGEO: Three-thirty A.M. is the usual hour for early-morning births. What is your month of birth?

HARLEQUIN: That is a matter of some dispute. Church records were kept by a dimwit named Cavicchio. In the birth record, he wrote October, in the baptismal record, April.

ARGEO: April, October: can't you be more precise?

HARLEQUIN: Precision is of no importance! I will tell you what is important: I came into the world. There is no event in the history of the world as important as that.

ARGEO: Everyone can make that statement.

HARLEQUIN: It is true in every case.

ARGEO: Are you a philosopher?

HARLEQUIN: I am a jester. I lampoon philosophers— and other so-called professionals. Shall we get back to the business of discovering what the stars have to say?

ARGEO consults a chart.

ARGEO: Your month of birth is uncertain: that makes it difficult. It is either April or October, sixth day, 3:30 A.M. April is Aries, whose element is fire and whose polarity is, unfortunately, negative. October is Libra, its element is air, its polarity is positive. To put it succinctly, if you were born in April, you are a dead duck; if in October, you are in luck. My advice is to arrange an October birthday.

ARGEO exits hastily.

HARLEQUIN: Arrange an October birthday! That fellow is a born comedian. His mistake is to take himself seriously.

COLOMBINA enters.

COLOMBINA: Fortune telling and astrology are of little use to you, Signore Harlequin.

HARLEQUIN: Who are you?

COLOMBINA: I am Colombina, healer of hearts.

HARLEQUIN: And what is your remedy?

COLOMBINA: You need something that affects you spiritually *and* physically: a love potion.

HARLEQUIN: I don't need a potion. I am already in love.

COLOMBINA: Ah, Signore, you deceive yourself. It is the adventure that enchants you, and you confuse this enchantment with love. True love radiates from your inner being. Swallow this potion in the presence of your beloved—at the right moment—and she will greet you with open arms.

HARLEQUIN takes vial, examines it

HARLEQUIN: How will I know the right moment?

COLOMBINA: I will give you a signal.

HARLEQUIN: What will the signal be?

COLOMBINA: A puff of confetti.

HARLEQUIN: Confetti?

COLOMBINA: Confetti.

HARLEQUIN: A puff?

COLOMBINA: A puff. You will not fail to see it.

HARLEQUIN drops a coin into COLOMBINA's extended hand. She extends her other hand, expecting yet another coin.

HARLEQUIN: I have paid you.

COLOMBINA: You paid for the love potion, but not the signal.

HARLEQUIN puts another coin in COLOMBINA'S hand. She exits.

HARLEQUIN: My fortune's been told, my stars have been read, I have a love potion. I am confused, abused, not amused—[Looks about]—and I won't be excused from jail if the constabulary catches up with me.

HARLEQUIN conceals himself in an obscure space.

SCENE NINE

Loud banging sounds are heard—that of a Viking battering ram pounding Arugula's west gate. Shouts and cries are heard at a distance as a message radiates throughout the town: "The Vikes are at our gates! The Vikes! The Vikes!" Enter PANTALONE, accompanied by a PAGE and BRAVADO.

PANTALONE: Captain Bravado, go quickly to the west gate before the Vikings knock it down. You are to deliver this message from Duke Lorenzo.

BRAVADO: Perhaps it would be best if the boy carried the message. I'll cover the east gate in case they try a flanking maneuver.

PANTALONE: Forget the east gate. Let me hear your declamation.

BRAVADO: I am authorized by Signore Pantalone, the Mayor of Arugula, to deliver this message from Lorenzo, Duke of Arugula, to King Olaf.

PANTALONE: Good. Stop trembling in your boots! This white flag will protect you from all harm. Now look confident.

> BRAVADO takes two brave steps. The Viking battering ram is heard again. Quivering, BRAVADO stops. PANTALONE'S stern brow sends him on his way. HARLEQUIN emerges from his hiding place and looks toward the castle.

HARLEQUIN: They have opened the gates of the castle. People are pouring out of it. This might be my chance.

PANTALONE: Who are you?

HARLEQUIN: A stranger passing through. I'll be on my way.

PANTALONE: A little more respect, please. I am Pantalone, Mayor of Arugula. Now who are you?

HARLEQUIN: I am Harlequin.

PANTALONE: Harlequin! I have a warrant from Magistrate Cassandro ordering you to leave town immediately under pain of—well, pain, lots of it. ... Wait! I'll give you a chance to mitigate your sentence. Join our militia and prepare to fight the Vikes—in case they reject the peace proposal.

HARLEQUIN: I am off to the nearest recruiting office.

HARLEQUIN exits.

PANTALONE: Where is the Duke? Too busy, I suppose, having sport with his concubines, leaving me to deal with the Vikings. ... If only the Duchess were in charge.

OLAF enters.

OLAF: Panty! I remember you from our last visit. I suppose you are still the mayor.

PANTALONE: No one else wants the job.

OLAF: I received the Duke's note. Your emissary must be half-starved. As soon as he placed the paper in my hand, he fainted.

PANTALONE: Captain Bravado has a condition called Chickinitis. ... I trust that your Majesty is here on vacation.

OLAF: My first order of business is to find two ladies from my court who are already here. Do you have any idea where they are?

PANTALONE: Scapino was seen escorting a lady and her attendant. [**To PAGE**] Find Scapino and have him bring the ladies here. [**PAGE runs off**] I expect that Duke Lorenzo will be arriving to greet you, King Olaf.

OLAF: The last time we came, he was the first to greet us.

PANTALONE: He has other preoccupations. [**Looks in the direction of the castle**] I can't believe my eyes: it is the Duchess, Isabella—dressed as a soldier. The Duke has never allowed her to leave the castle.

Enter ISABELLA

ISABELLA: Greetings Signore Pantalone. Greetings, King Olaf. Assuming that you do not come in a warlike spirit, I welcome you to Arugula.

OLAF: And if I am in a warlike spirit—

ISABELLA: I will lead our army against you.

OLAF: General Isabella, another Joan of Arc. I wouldn't fight her, and I won't fight you.

> **Quarreling is heard off stage. PANTALONE looks in that direction.**

PANTALONE: It is Scapino—arguing with Ottavio. I'll fetch them.

> **PANTALONE exits.**

OLAF: Have you decided to take up a military career?

ISABELLA: The uniform is a disguise. Running off with a group of soldiers, my escape was not noticed.

OLAF: The soldiers helped you—

ISABELLA: Willingly. I lead their drills. They would go to war at my command.

OLAF: Where is Lorenzo?

ISABELLA: He is with his barber; then he will see his tailor and grooming assistant. Castle gossips say that he hopes to pluck up a Nordic daisy.

OLAF: The Nordic daisy is my wife.

ISABELLA: You have arrived in time to prevent the worst from happening.

OLAF: Sieglinde is an autonomous being. The decision will be hers.

ISABELLA: You are a wise man, Olaf. She may waver, but, if she has sense, she will choose you.

OLAF: I hope so.

Enter SCAPINO. Bowing deeply, nervously, he addresses OLAF.

SCAPINO: Welcome back to Arugula, your Majesty.

OLAF: You fleeced me the last time I was here, Scapino.

SCAPINO: It was an error, sir—a misunderstanding. I will make restitution.

OLAF: Be sure you do. It will not be forgotten.

SCAPINO: It will be done, sir.

SIEGLINDE, HELGA and OTTAVIO enter.

OLAF: Who is the gentleman?

ISABELLA: He is Ottavio, who was my betrothed.

OTTAVIO: Isabella, forgive me, but I had lost hope. I have just today met Lady Dorinda and her lady in waiting, Dina.

OLAF: Dorinda! Dina! I know them as Sieglinde and Helga.

OTTAVIO: Is the Lady Dorinda—beg pardon, Sieglinde—related to you?

OLAF: She is my wife.

OTTAVIO: Oh! I am deceived!

ISABELLA: Deceived! Such piety! Be honest, Ottavio: you saw an opportunity for love-making with a very attractive lady.

OTTAVIO: I protest! My intentions were honorable.

ISABELLA: Honorable intentions! What has happened to you Ottavio? Where is the irreverent young man who wooed me, who told me a thousand delightful lies?

OTTAVIO: I was myself then. I am no longer myself. I have learned to live in fear. Duke Lorenzo's spies watch my every move. Your father wishes me dead, and he has considerable influence. [**To OLAF**] This encounter will be reported. I would prefer to make it as brief as possible. With your permission, I shall withdraw.

OLAF signals approval. OTTAVIO exits.

ISABELLA: Ottavio has been turned into a shadow of his once beautiful self. How sad.

OLAF: Well Sieglinde, are you enjoying your Italian vacation?

SIEGLINDE: I was until you interrupted our tour. May we resume it?

OLAF: Not yet. Let me introduce you to Isabella, Duchess of Arugula. I suspect that you and she have something in common.

ISABELLA: I am no longer a Duchess. I renounce the title. I have escaped Lorenzo's castle. I will not go back.

SIEGLINDE: We do have something in common: I, too, have escaped from a castle.

ISABELLA: That is brave, but I note that you are dressed fashionably and have a serving girl to attend to your needs. If you are to make a serious escape, you must be prepared to wear ordinary clothes, cheap jewelry and work as a shopkeeper.

SIEGLINDE: For the moment I wish only to enjoy the Italian sun.

PANTALONE enters, excited.

PANTALONE: Duchess, your father has learned of your escape. He is looking for a magistrate who will order you to return to the castle. I regret to say it, but the law will sustain him.

ISABELLA: If my father comes near me, I will greet him with a sword. If the magistrates oppose me, I will lead the army against them.

Enter HARLEQUIN, carrying a foot soldier's pike and wearing a militia cap. Self-absorbed, he notices no one.

ISABELLA: There is a soldier I don't recognize. Who is he?

PANTALONE: He is a commedia character, Harlequin— also called Harley. He is a wanderer, a man who lives by his wits, and who, in love, is witless.

ISABELLA: What is his role in the commedia?

PANTALONE: His role is to expose every human folly, and there is no folly that he himself does not exhibit. He is a comic character, never really serious, yet the most serious of men. I sent him, on his honor, to join the militia. He has done so.

ISABELLA: That is to his credit.

PANTALONE: True. Nonetheless, I will have to order his arrest. He is presently acting in defiance of a warrant issued by Magistrate Cassandro, ordering him to leave Arugula.

ISABELLA: Allow me to ask for his pardon. I will intercede with Signore Cassandro. [**Calls**] Harley.

HARLEQUIN: Who calls?

ISABELLA: Me.

HARLEQUIN: [**Approaches Isabella**] I must be dreaming for I would swear that the soldier standing before me is Isabella.

ISABELLA: I am Isabella.

A puff of confetti floats in the air.

HARLEQUIN: Ah! Colombina's signal.

HARLEQUIN is about to swallow the love potion.

ISABELLA: Don't take it! You have no need of potions. You have passion enough without them.

HARLEQUIN: I have spent three years searching for you, Isabella; now that I see you standing before me, I realize that I am not worthy of you.

ISABELLA: Why?

HARLEQUIN: I cannot aspire to your nobility.

ISABELLA: I have renounced nobility.

HARLEQUIN: Look at me, Isabella. I am a jester, an actor—a rascal. I do not possess the graces and charms that you will surely expect.

ISABELLA: By every social yardstick, you are unsuitable. Your origin is the theater, thought to be vulgar; yet men and women of all classes—even queens and kings—eagerly await your performances. The commedia troupes that visit the castle have been the only light in my dreary life.

HARLEQUIN: There are lots of dreary lives. Marry a rogue and you will find that out.

ISABELLA: I will marry for love, and my love will make my rogue honest.

HARLEQUIN: I hope—for your sake—that you are not thinking of me.

ISABELLA: You have pursued me for three years. I have waited three years. You are the man.

HARLEQUIN: I would be a bad choice.

ISABELLA: There is no talking me out of it, Harley.

HARLEQUIN: What am I to do?

ISABELLA: Submit.

HARLEQUIN: Who is to submit?

ISABELLA: You.

HARLEQUIN: Is there a me? I have innumerable masks. Which is the original? I have lost track.

ISABELLA: I'll help you find the original. Who am I to choose from?

HARLEQUIN: Doctor Hippocraso, who discourses eloquently on the spleen and the liver; Lelo, a practical joker; Boraccio, a magician whose tricks confuse him and delight the audience. In a light-hearted mood, I am Turchetto, a Turkish eunuch; in a military mood, I am Captain Cocodrillo, who will tell in grisly detail how he subdued the Eastern heathens. I am born anew as Trinio, son of the god Mercury, who walks on stilts so as not to breathe the common air. I stay close to the ground as Woof, the dog who is smarter than his master. On solemn occasions, I am Bonifacio, Bishop of Bopaloopoo; on royal occasions, I am Stefano, the only Italian King of Poland. I am a pickpocket, a beggar, a vagabond, a clown, a bungling cop. I play the fool—a rich fool, a poor fool, a fool's fool. In sum, I am a will o' the wisp, a chameleon whose very existence is in doubt.

ISABELLA: You are holding out on me Harley. You haven't mentioned the lover.

HARLEQUIN: Oh, him. He is a scoundrel known as Don Giovanni. Have nothing to do with him.

ISABELLA: Don Giovanni is my choice.

HARLEQUIN: He will love you and leave you, as he does all women.

ISABELLA: When he does, good riddance. The real Harley will remain.

HARLEQUIN: There is no real Harley.

ISABELLA: Oh, but there is. He is the constant element in every character. Your time is up, Harley. You have no choice but to submit.

> HARLEQUIN makes a grand gesture of submission. He and ISABELLA embrace.

HARLEQUIN: Come Isabella, let us leave the stage to sincere lovers.

> HARLEQUIN and ISABELLA exit.

Scene Ten

SCAPINO: Sincere? Who do you suppose he meant?

PANTALONE: He meant you, Scapino. His eyes were aimed right at you when he spoke the word.

SCAPINO: Oh, no—no, no, no. I have numerous—well, a few—failings, but Sincerity is not one of them.

PANTALONE: I sense that even a king can be disarmed by love. Come, let us stand aside.

SCAPINO and PANTALONE stand aside.

OLAF: Yes, even a king is disarmed by love; and now he must confess it. I have come to love you, Sieglinde, I still do. But if you cannot feel love for me I will let you go.

SIEGLINDE: You were not my choice, Olaf. You were my father's choice. I was engaged to a man I never met—a pawn in a political alliance between two kingdoms. I have resented that.

OLAF: I don't blame you. ... If you decide to leave me, I will understand.

SIEGLINDE: I suppose it would be easy for you to let me go. I need only utter the words: I wish to leave you.

OLAF: Those words would break my heart. But if life with me breaks your heart, I have no right to hold you.

SIEGLINDE: How long do you plan to stay in Arugula?

OLAF: There are affairs of state that need my attention. I can only spare a week.

SIEGLINDE: I will answer you by the end of the week.

OLAF: Scapino, find us a first-class inn—at a fair price.

SCAPINO: I will get the best possible price. I will make sure you have the innkeeper's best prices for wine and food; and I will waive my commission.

OLAF: Signore Pantalone, send a message to Lorenzo: I won't stay in his castle. I will pay him a courtesy visit tomorrow.

SIEGLINDE: I will forgo the honor of making that visit.

This remark surprises and delights OLAF.

SCAPINO: Well, now, all is settled—until it becomes unsettled. Before that happens, let's sing, dance and be merry. Our lives will end soon enough, and there is neither dancing, nor singing, nor love—nor commissions— to be had in the grave.

Exeunt all, singing, dancing and making merry.

FADE TO BLACK

Scene Eleven

HUSBAND and WIFE at breakfast table. HUSBAND reads newspaper, WIFE sips her coffee in a dreamy mood.

HUSBAND: Market is up ... Weather, sunny ... What do you know: after winning four elimination games, the high school hockey team won the state championship.

WIFE: Bravo. ... Is there a crumpet?

HUSBAND: There is one left. It has your name on it: raspberry.

WIFE: My name is not raspberry.

HUSBAND: In that case, I will eat it.

WIFE: Don't you dare.

HUSBAND passes plate to WIFE. She takes the crumpet, he returns to his newspaper.

HUSBAND: Look at this—a challenge quiz in the paper. How long does it take sunlight to reach Pluto? Before we started this dream business, I could figure that out in my head. Now I can't do it: my internal calculator is defunct. Those dreams have ruined me.

WIFE: The mathematical wizard has discovered his other self—a commedia actor named Harley. Passion replaces the calculator. I like it.

HUSBAND: What did Isabella do for you?

WIFE: Not much—in fact, nothing. I don't like soldiering. And I didn't like that business of wearing cheap jewelry and working as a shopkeeper. My sympathies were with Sieglinde. She started as a spoiled girl and matured into a woman.

HUSBAND: Do you suppose there will be another dream?

WIFE: The next story is quite exciting. It will involve Brighella.

HUSBAND: Brighella! An unrepentant rogue! He is to be the hero! Are you sure?

WIFE: In life, I am your wife. In my dream life I am a commedia actress. I flirted with the company manager and he showed me the next dream's scenario.

HUSBAND: Flirted—?

WIFE: Flirted.

FADE TO BLACK

Dreams

TALES OF THE COMMEDIA DELL'ARTE

Part Two: Brighella

Time & Place

Venice, 16th Century

Settings

A small park with shrubs and benches
A patio in a residential courtyard
A room in the Doge's Palace

Scene Summary [2]

Prelude: Two Jesters, Constable
One: Brighella, Constable, Stefano, Lucia
Two: Beatrice, Niccolo
Three: Beatrice, Brighella
Four: Colombina, Brighella
Five: Doge, Leandro, Fulminato
Six: Commendatore, Pompeo, Brighella
Seven: Fulminato, Constable, Brighella
Eight: Colombina, Pompeo
Nine: Beatrice, Leandro
Ten: Stefano, Fabrizio, Lucia, Rosaura
Eleven: Lucia
Twelve: Beatrice, Pompeo
Thirteen: Brighella, Constable
Fourteen: Doge, Brighella, Lucia, Leandro, Fulminato
Fifteen: Doge, Beatrice, Leandro, Pompeo
Epilogue: Brighella, Constable, Lucia

---

[2] Note: With part doubling—making use of masks and simple costumes (capes, hats, glasses, beards, etc.)—all parts can be played by seven to nine performers. Scenes flow into each other, time is elastic.

Prelude

A small park with two benches and a cluster of bushes at the rear. A funeral procession enters on one side of the stage, moves solemnly, and exits the other side. The procession is led by a deacon with a prayer book. He is followed by two pallbearers who carry the casket, using handles extending from front and rear. Two jesters and a constable follow the casket.

FIRST JESTER: Death is the end of a man's sorrows.

SECOND JESTER: Death is the end of a man's joys.

CONSTABLE: Death is *not* the end of a man's mischief. The next generation inherits it.

The funeral procession exits.

Scene One

The park. A moonlit scene. A voice is heard off-stage, at a distance.

VOICE: Stop thief!

Enter **BRIGHELLA** in great haste. He hides a cape in a space hidden by the bushes. He removes his outer garments—blouse, breeches, doublet—and hides them. The undressing reveals simple peasant clothing: a white cotton blouse and pants with green trim that had been worn under the aristocratic garments. He puts a necklace around his neck and covers it with his blouse. A man, an aristocrat to judge by his dress, enters. He walks hastily, taking pains to keep his face covered. Upon his approach, Brighella bows—the commoner's traditional courtesy. The two men collide

BRIGHELLA: I beg your pardon, sir.

THE MAN: You bungler!

BRIGHELLA helps The MAN arrange his cloak

BRIGHELLA: I was trying to extend a courtesy. It was my fault.

THE MAN: If I had time, I would have you whipped.

THE MAN looks to the rear, then exits hastily. BRIGHELLA displays a purse that he filched from the man's cloak. He removes a note from the purse, reads.

BRIGHELLA: "Beautiful lady Rosalie, how grateful I am to thee." Fancy stationery.

BRIGHELLA examines another section of the purse. Pulls out a batch of bills.

BRIGHELLA: A nice haul.

STEFANO: [Heard from off stage] I am getting tired. My heart ...

CONSTABLE: [Heard from off stage] Let's try the lovers park. It is just ahead.

BRIGHELLA hastily tosses the purse into the space behind the bushes then adopts the pose of a man out for night air. CONSTABLE enters, followed by COUNT STEFANO.

STEFANO: There he is. That's your man.

BRIGHELLA: I beg your pardon—

STEFANO: Look at him, trying to brazen it out.

CONSTABLE: I recognize him. He is Brighella, a famous commedia actor—a rogue on and off stage. He has been charged with a hundred crimes, convicted of none. Where Brighella has been, suspicion lingers; but hard evidence is never found.

STEFANO: Ah-hah! A known criminal. I saw him as he fled.

BRIGHELLA: Fleeing from where?

STEFANO: My wife's boudoir.

BRIGHELLA: Are you sure you want to make this public?

STEFANO: You stole my wife's necklace.

CONSTABLE: Excuse me, Count Stefano, but you said that the thief was dressed as an aristocrat. This man is wearing commoner's clothes.

STEFANO: I— I don't understand it ...

> A woman's voice is heard. "Have you got him?"
> COUNTESS LUCIA enters, approaches BRIGHELLA.

LUCIA: So Leandro, I have caught up with you. You scoundrel!

CONSTABLE: This man is Brighella, not Leandro. And his clothing is not as you described.

LUCIA: Wha-a-t? Not Leandro!

BRIGHELLA: The man you want passed by a few minutes ago. He was running as fast as he could—in that direction.

LUCIA: [Aside] That voice! [To Constable] There is no need to go running off. We have caught the deceiver. He stole my necklace. [Runs her hands over Brighella's blouse] A thief and a deceiver! Come, rogue, give me my necklace. [Pulls necklace out from under BRIGHELLA's blouse] Ah-hah! Here it is.

CONSTABLE: Caught with the evidence. Brighella will finally go to jail. I might get a promotion out of this.

BRIGHELLA: I am sorry to delay your promotion, Constable, but this is not the lady's necklace: it is my own.

CONSTABLE: It is hard to believe that you wear a woman's necklace.

BRIGHELLA: I wear it to honor the memory of my dear mother, who gave it to me on her deathbed. "Wear that necklace," she said, "and I will smile down on you from Heaven."

LUCIA: He is a liar! It is my necklace.

BRIGHELLA: Perhaps, if I might have a word with the lady, we might save embarrassment.

CONSTABLE: Does the lady agree?

LUCIA thinks it over, an exchange of glances with BRIGHELLA

LUCIA: Yes, I do.

STEFANO: Just a moment! This is very improper! Lucia, remember your social status: you are a countess, that man is a commoner. Worse, he is a thief—worse yet, an actor!

LUCIA: Even worse, a deceiver! I want the pleasure of sending him to jail.

CONSTABLE: You have five minutes.

LUCIA and BRIGHELLA step aside, begin a sotto voce conversation.

CONSTABLE: [To STEFANO] How did you come upon the scene?

STEFANO: I heard a noise coming from my wife's bed chamber. When I entered, the thief was escaping out a window. My wife was on her bed—flat on her back. She said the villain threw her there.

CONSTABLE: Flat on her back ... and the lady is willing to parley ... Let's see if we can follow the conversation.

BRIGHELLA removes a handkerchief from his sleeve.

CONSTABLE: Brighella is tearful ... He doesn't want to go to jail .... She says, I don't give a damn! .... He is telling her about his children who depend on him for food and shelter ...

STEFANO: He has children?

CONSTABLE: Six that he admits to—in various parts of town. ... The lady is not moved.

STEFANO: Of course not. ... What is the rogue up to now?

CONSTABLE: Brighella is describing a scene. ... An object here ... a door there ... a window ... a bed. I see what he is up to: he is reminding the lady that he has intimate knowledge of her boudoir.

STEFANO: It's a bluff. He won't fool Lucia with that.

CONSTABLE: He is rapping something ... a hammer? ... Ah! It is a gavel. A judge calling a court to order. A crowd ... a big crowd. ... They are to witness a trial. ... Brighella is called to testify. His hand is on the Bible. ... The whole truth, nothing but the truth ... He steals a glance at the lady. ... His expression says: I have no choice but to tell the truth.

STEFANO: The truth! My wife! I do not believe it!

LUCIA: You louse!!!

STEFANO: Good heavens!

CONSTABLE: Now Brighella is making his pitch. ... He is showing her the necklace ... he is pointing to individual stones ... the cut of this one, the shape of that one, the size of the emerald ... The lady is outraged. ... I get it: she is to say that the necklace is not hers.

STEFANO: [Faint, unsteady on his feet] Has it come to this? ... Oh, my heart.

CONSTABLE: Brighella says be calm and listen to the rest of his proposal. ... Out of the goodness of his heart ... he will give her his necklace ... the one he got from his mother in Heaven. Very clever. The Countess gets her necklace back, she is saved from a scandalous trial, and Brighella can't be accused of stealing. ... The deal is sealed: here they come.

LUCIA: Constable, I have examined the necklace carefully. It is not mine.

STEFANO: It most certainly is yours. I recognize it.

LUCIA: You do not know it as intimately as I do. There is a resemblance to be sure, but the emerald is too small, other stones are cut differently. It is not mine, but Signore Brighella has agreed to let me have his necklace as compensation for my loss.

CONSTABLE: Do you agree, Brighella?

BRIGHELLA: [A glance toward heaven] Forgive me mother. [To CONSTABLE] I agree.

STEFANO: We are getting an inferior necklace.

CONSTABLE: I don't think you need concern yourself about that, sir. Brighella has once again beaten the rap. There goes my promotion. ... Shall we be on our way?

STEFANO and CONSTABLE exit. LUCIA looks back at BRIGHELLA, then exits.

BRIGHELLA: **[Addresses audience]** A failure! If you have to give back the object, you have failed. Countess Lucia has beaten me. It is rare that the woman joins the pursuit: that was my undoing. ... She owes me something: I did her good service. Oh how she squeezed me and cried, "I love you, I love you, I love you." I hit the jackpot with her. As for Leandro, I borrowed his name and his clothes, but he has no reason to complain. Once he was known as "Don Juan," visiting the boudoirs of eager women. He went to a monastery, got religion, and is now known as "The Monk." I am restoring his better name.

OLIVIA enters.

OLIVIA: Oh, there you are! You had me worried.

BRIGHELLA: You had reason to worry. I nearly went to jail. My wits saved me. But I had to give up the jewels. Rotten luck! They would have fetched a fortune. With that, Olivia, I would have doubled your pay.

OLIVIA: For a housekeeper, pay raises are always in the future.

BRIGHELLA: Don't complain. I pay you twice as much as the nobility pay their servants.

OLIVIA: When you work for a man who is likely to end up in jail, twice as much is only half-enough.

BRIGHELLA: Take Leandro's clothes and put them away. I will be home later.

BRIGHELLA makes a bundle of Leandro's clothes and hands them, with the purse, to OLIVIA.

OLIVIA: [Holds up purse] Whose purse is this?

BRIGHELLA: A gentleman gave it to me.

OLIVIA: Willingly?

BRIGHELLA: Of course not.

OLIVIA: There is a name inside it. I can't read.

OLIVIA hands the purse to BRIGHELLA. He examines it.

BRIGHELLA: Duke d'Amaro. He is the Doge's son-in-law.

OLIVIA: A relative of the Doge! I will soon be unemployed. I will not attend your hanging.

BRIGHELLA: Duke d'Amaro will hold his tongue. If the loss is discovered, he will say that he lost it or that brigands took it from him. He doesn't dare admit that he was in a lady's boudoir, running no doubt from an angry husband—an aristocrat, very likely a close pal of the Doge.

Voices are heard approaching. BRIGHELLA waves OLIVIA off. She exits, carrying clothes and purse. BRIGHELLA conceals himself behind the bushes.

SCENE TWO

BEATRICE and NICCOLO enter. An embrace, a kiss.

NICCOLO: Oh, Beatrice, I have so much love to give you—

BEATRICE: Dearest Niccolo, I will accept your love joy-fully—when we are married.

NICCOLO: When we are married! Every delight is postponed until we are married. We will never be mar-ried—not as long as your father is alive. If I meet him in the street he points a finger at me and declares that he will never have me for a son-in-law.

BEATRICE: You must not despair. I will reject Pompeo, the man Papa has chosen for me. Then Papa will relent and I shall choose my husband.

NICCOLO: Your father is not the relenting type. Our love is doomed, unless— We have one chance, one only: if you were expecting a child your father would have no choice but to relent.

BEATRICE is shocked at the suggestion.

NICCOLO: We'd be married long before the child is born.

BEATRICE: Every bachelor says that—just before he boards the ship that will take him to Sicily or Turkey.

NICCOLO: I protest! I am sincere.

BEATRICE slaps NICCOLO's face.

BEATRICE: I am deeply offended by your suggestion! You treat me as you would a street walker.

NICCOLO: I protest! I am a lover—a desperate one, but one who respects you.

NICCOLO attempts to hug BEATRICE. She pushes him off.

BEATRICE: Papa is expecting me.

NICCOLO: [Angry] Go, go to Papa!

NICCOLO wheels about and departs.

SCENE THREE

BRIGHELLA enters, BEATRICE catches sight of him.

BEATRICE: Who are you? Were you eavesdropping?

BRIGHELLA: Eavesdropping! Never. My mother in heaven would not forgive me. I am simply out for a stroll.

BEATRICE: What did you hear?

BRIGHELLA: Voices—a man's and a woman's.

BEATRICE: What else?

BRIGHELLA: I heard what sounded like a slap—a rather loud one.

BEATRICE displays her hand in slapping mode.

BEATRICE: You heard the voice of conscience. It brings a rising passion to an abrupt halt.

BRIGHELLA: Why not let the passion be fulfilled?

BEATRICE: One hour of pleasure can cost years of unhappiness. Go about town and watch the girls who are round with child. The one with the wedding ring is content, the one without it is melancholy. Her parents are ashamed of her, no man will marry her, she is scorned by society. Most often she lives with a dour aunt who says to her every day, "You brought it on yourself."

BRIGHELLA: A sad fate. But they say that a pregnancy occurs only once in fifteen attempts.

BEATRICE: The first attempt has as good a chance as the other fourteen.

BRIGHELLA: True, but one in fifteen is a good gamble.

BEATRICE: It is no gamble when only one of the gamblers stands to take the loss.

BRIGHELLA: I sense that you are too defensive about life and love. You fancy that the voice of conscience has saved you from an unhappy fate. But you might be making a bad gamble. You have no idea what you have lost.

BEATRICE: What have I lost?

BRIGHELLA: Sheer ecstasy! Pure delight. It comes only when love is shared with another person.

BEATRICE: I long to have that experience—after I am married.

BRIGHELLA: Fatal words! You delay happiness now and you will delay it again and again, even after you are married.

> BEATRICE is quiet, contemplative: she has thought of this possibility. A passing MUSICIAN enters.

BRIGHELLA: Ah, music! We are in luck. Or is it fate? Yes, I think it must be fate. [To MUSICIAN] Surely you have a dance tune in your repertoire.

> BRIGHELLA hands a coin to the MUSICIAN, who begins to play.

BRIGHELLA: [To Beatrice] May I have this dance?

> They dance. BRIGHELLA speaks slowly, seductively.

BRIGHELLA: You dance gracefully. ... You have no idea how beautiful you are. Nor do I. ... Your real beauty is bottled up inside. ... It won't be released until you have shared ecstasy with a lover. You will then be a woman in full blossom, a woman who radiates beauty. ... It would give me great happiness to introduce you to the joys of love—to bring out your hidden beauty, the goddess within you.

> **BEATRICE seems to be enchanted, or shall we say intrigued. BRIGHELLA has led her to the bushes. The last turn of their dance takes them behind the bushes. Shaking of the bushes would indicate that BRIGHELLA is being rather aggressive. A loud SLAP is heard. Angry, BEATRICE emerges, pulling her dress above her shoulders. She exits. MUSICIAN exits. BRIGHELLA emerges from the bush, a hand print on his cheek.**

BRIGHELLA: What a conscience!

SCENE FOUR

> **A residential courtyard. COLOMBINA is sweeping a patio. BRIGHELLA enters. Bemused, he listens to COLOMBINA'S lament (addressed to the audience).**

COLOMBINA: The life of a servant is no life, especially when there are six incompetent souls and a dog to look after. The master calls: "Colombina, where is my book?" I run up three flights and find it two feet from his hand. The mistress calls out, "Colombina, my corset." I run down three flights: the corset is at her feet. Then the chorus gets going. "Colombina, where is my shawl?" "Colombina, my slippers." "Colombina, don't forget to walk the dog—and don't let him jump into the canal." The young gentleman drops his cuff pin into the canal and expects me to dive in and fish it out. "Find it yourself," I said, and shoved him into the canal. Then I went straight to the master and said, "I quit." He refused to take my resignation. "Colombina," he says, "you are neglecting your duties. First, fish my son out of the canal, then prepare my bath. After that you will need to change Auntie's bed pan, then fix supper." ... I'll fix them: I'll cook the stew in the bed pan.

BRIGHELLA: That is a delightful trick.

COLOMBINA: Well, well, Brighella. Long time, no see. What mischief brings you my way?

BRIGHELLA: A little intrigue.

COLOMBINA: Are you paying? I mean cash. Kisses won't do.

BRIGHELLA: Colombina! I thought you loved me.

COLOMBINA: I do love you. I also love oysters and roast goose. Cash in my purse puts oysters and goose on my plate.

BRIGHELLA: You shall have cash. I have devised a new commedia scenario for you: you will play Madame Zanobia, clairvoyant. She is consulted by kings and queens. Her predictions saved the Russian empire.

COLOMBINA: What is Madame Zanobia to do?

BRIGHELLA: A vixen slapped my face. I must be avenged—and of course make a profit.

COLOMBINA: How?

BRIGHELLA: By getting the vixen married to a man she despises—her father's choice. His name is Pompeo, a dimwit who happens to be the richest man in Venice. His purse will supply the profits.

COLOMBINA: I will need ten scudi—paid in advance.

BRIGHELLA: Money, money, money: that's all you hear these days. Venetians have become too materialistic. I have three scudi in my purse. When is your next day off?

COLOMBINA: Saturday. I will need seven more scudi before I say a word to you.

BRIGHELLA: Call on me Saturday.

BRIGHELLA exits. Voices are heard from the house: "Colombina." She counts on her fingers until six voices are heard. She pauses to hear one last voice: "bow-wow," then enters the house.

SCENE FIVE

A room in the Doge's palace. The DOGE is seated at a desk thumbing through a clutch of letters. LEANDRO enters.

LEANDRO: Good morning, your Excellency.

DOGE: It would be a better morning if I did not have all these complaints about you, Leandro: letters from the most prominent men in Venice who say that you are playing your old Don Juan game—visiting their wives' boudoirs. This time you have added a new twist: taking a valuable souvenir as you leave.

LEANDRO: That last item proves that I am not the man. I have no need of souvenirs: I have my own fortune. The guilty man is a clever burglar.

DOGE: The man wears a cloak and garments bearing your insignia. He gives his name as Leandro.

LEANDRO: The lady's boudoir is dark, he wears a mask—a black mask of fine cloth like I used to wear. Thus, he passes for me. As for the cloak and garments, they were stolen from me.

DOGE: Your evidence is circumstantial; your past weighs heavily against you. Five years ago you were known as Don Juan. These same men demanded the death sentence.

LEANDRO: Hypocrites! Every one of them has a mistress, some have two mistresses.

DOGE: A gentleman will gladly cuckold another gentleman; when it happens to him, he is outraged. I didn't care about their opinions: I was concerned about you, Leandro. I was hoping you would take on political responsibilities— serve Venice. When you stood before me five years ago enraged husbands wanted you hanged. But my objective was not vengeance: it was to bring you to your senses. I sentenced you to live two years in the most austere monastery in the Venetian Republic. When you returned you swore that you were a man transformed.

LEANDRO: I spoke truthfully. The friars taught me to nourish my soul, to live a life of the spirit. I committed myself to a bachelor's life. I have lived up to that pledge.

DOGE: This requires further investigation. You have the freedom of the city, but do not leave Venice.

> **LEANDRO bows and exits. The DOGE rings a bell. FULMINATO, Venice's Chief of Security, enters.**

FULMINATO: Your Excellency.

DOGE: Fulminato, it is possible that someone has stolen Leandro's clothing. Disguised as Leandro he gains access to women's bed chambers. He then makes off with valuable jewels.

FULMINATO: [A guffaw] From what I have heard he steals other treasures as well.

DOGE: We are only interested in the clothing and stolen jewelry. I want you to find the man and arrest him.

FULMINATO: I will mobilize the force, attack every angle of inquiry, pursue every lead; I will enlist spies, and—do I need to dredge the canals?

DOGE: It is unlikely that the man you are looking for is at the bottom of a canal.

FULMINATO: Very well, no canals. I promise your Excellency—

DOGE: Hadn't you better get started.

FULMINATO: Immediately, promptly, with full devotion to Venice and your Excellency.

FULMINATO bows and exits.

SCENE SIX

Enter COMMENDATORE GALLEGGIGANTI and POMPEO. BRIGHELLA, in the guise of a soothsayer, enters from the other side. He watches from a distance.

COMMENDATORE: I have three daughters. Two followed my wishes in the matter of selecting a husband; they are happy and have brought me grandchildren. But Beatrice defies me, though I most certainly know what is best for her.

POMPEO: She treats me—her future husband—with contempt. She even threatened to slap my face. She calls her slapping hand the voice of conscience.

COMMENDATORE: She will come around. You are the best man for her, Pompeo, no doubt about that. ... Oh, by the way, have you heard from your lawyer about the dowry?

POMPEO: He tells me that I can waive the dowry. My mother is of the opinion that you chose me to marry Beatrice because I am the only one rich enough to let you off without paying a dowry. She calls you Commendatore Skinflint.

COMMENDATORE: I chose you because of your manly qualities, your noble character. You are the one man in Venice who has the Roman brow. As for the dowry, I'd gladly pay it, but my investments have been doing badly.

BRIGHELLA: Pardon the intrusion, sir, but I recognize you: Commendatore Galleggiganti, hero of the last Turkish war. You rode your steed so valiantly in the victory parade. It made us all proud to be Venetians. ... Ah, but time goes on: civic pride gives way to other things. Prices and taxes go up, there is more crime, family life suffers, children rebel against their parents...

COMMENDATORE: Were you listening to our conversation?

BRIGHELLA: I couldn't help but overhear a few words. It occurred to me that I might be of service to you.

COMMENDATORE: You—a man in rags. What sort of service could you possibly do for me?

BRIGHELLA: My profession is soothsayer.

COMMENDATORE: A soothsayer! They were around in ancient times—predicted the future.

BRIGHELLA: We don't predict the future: we sense impending disaster. Caesar ignored the soothsayer and it cost him his life. I am a poor man—I have known hunger—yet my advice is gold.

COMMENDATORE: What sort of golden advice do you have for me?

BRIGHELLA: I advise you to let your daughter marry the man she loves.

COMMENDATORE: Nonsense! It is foolish to marry for love. Besides, if I consent to your proposal, I will lose prestige, my public reputation. I will be laughed at everywhere.

BRIGHELLA: When you are older—when prestige is an old, tattered flag—a happy daughter will cheer you up; an unhappy daughter will be an unsmiling crab—a scold.

COMMENDATORE: Like a wife—

BRIGHELLA: Worse.

POMPEO: If Beatrice is to marry for love, who will she marry?

BRIGHELLA: The man her father has chosen.

POMPEO: That's me! But how is it to be done?

BRIGHELLA: She is not seeing your merits. If she is determined to marry for love, then she must come to love you.

POMPEO: I see the strategy. This man may be in rags, but he understands a good deal.

COMMENDATORE: I don't like this win-the-girl-over strategy. Beatrice is a willful girl, and—like a wild pony—she must be broken.

BRIGHELLA: Willful girls will one day rule the world.

COMMENDATORE: And the world will be worse off for it.

BRIGHELLA: The world is not destined to be well off.

POMPEO: I like the idea of getting Beatrice to fall in love with me. How am I to do it?

BRIGHELLA: I am not the one to advise you in that matter. Go to the little park favored by lovers. There you will find an incomparable psychic, Madame Zanobia. She will help you.

POMPEO: I am on my way without delay.

BRIGHELLA: Sirs, I am a poor man who has not eaten today. Will you help me out?

POMPEO: The Commendatore will help you. I can't spare a moment.

> POMPEO dashes off. COMMENDATORE puts a coin in BRIGHELLA's hand and marches off. BRIGHELLA examines the coin and throws it away.

BRIGHELLA: Skinflint!

SCENE SEVEN

The park. Enter FULMINATO and the CONSTABLE.

FULMINATO: You say that you know who the Leandro bandit is.

CONSTABLE: Yes. It is Brighella. It was he who tried to steal Countess Lucia's necklace.

FULMINATO: Who is this Brig-fella? I never heard of him.

CONSTABLE: You are Venice's chief of security and you never heard of Brighella! I can't believe it.

FULMINATO: This Brig-fella is a detail. I leave details to my subordinates. Do you know where he lives?

CONSTABLE: No, but it should not be difficult for an efficient security agency to find out.

FULMINATO: Do you doubt our efficiency?

CONSTABLE: Well—

FULMINATO: My men are all about us. Can you see them?

CONSTABLE: No ...

FULMINATO: You can't see them: that's efficiency. ... Men!

VOICES: Agent POOF reporting: I am here ... Agent POF reporting: ready for action .... Agent PUFF reporting: armed and ready ...

CONSTABLE: I'll be damned! I still can't see them.

FULMINATO: Men! I have met a police officer who is hot on the trail of this Brig-fella.

Enter BRIGHELLA in a police uniform

BRIGHELLA: I know where he is at all times: he cannot evade me. But I cannot arrest him.

FULMINATO: We will help you. You have done excellent work! What is your name?

BRIGHELLA: O'Reilly.

FULMINATO: Men, follow O'Reilly.

FULMINATO, BRIGHELLA and the voices exit. The CONSTABLE, in a fit of laughter, remains behind.

CONSTABLE: Bravo, rogue!

SCENE EIGHT

The park. COLOMBINA is set up as a fortune teller: a table, a crystal ball. She is practicing wand waves. Enter POMPEO. A sound of wood on wood

as COLOMBINA's wand accidentally strikes his head. POMPEO does not notice it.

COLOMBINA: Oh, I beg your pardon.

POMPEO: For what?

COLOMBINA: My wand struck your head.

POMPEO: It did?

COLOMBINA: You didn't feel it?

POMPEO: No, I—ouch! I just felt it.

COLOMBINA: How odd.

POMPEO: My condition was given a Latin name—though I can't remember it. In language we understand it is a delayed response. My nervous system runs counter-clockwise. A normal system runs clockwise.

COLOMBINA: I take it that you wish to consult me. What is your name?

POMPEO: Pompeo.

COLOMBINA: Why are you here?

POMPEO: I am engaged to Beatrice—that is I am her father's choice. Still she is coy. I am desperate to know if she will be part of my future.

COLOMBINA: Have you written a love poem?

POMPEO: I am no good at poetry.

COLOMBINA: Have you given her gifts?

POMPEO: I gave her a box of chocolates.

COLOMBINA: You need help. Luckily, you have come to the right place. My policy is cash in advance.

POMPEO fishes a coin out of his purse and drops it in COLOMBINA's cash box. COLOMBINA tosses the coin back at him.

COLOMBINA: Are you a pauper? I am Madame Zanobia, consultant to kings and queens. I deal only in gold coins.

POMPEO: Beg pardon, I didn't know.

POMPEO drops a gold coin in the cash box. COLOMBINA remains huffy. POMPEO puts a second gold coin in the box. COLOMBINA closes the lid on the box, sits, and signals POMPEO that he is to sit opposite her.

COLOMBINA: Now we begin. Do not move or make a sound.

COLOMBINA's concentration is accompanied by moans and wailing until she reaches what seems to be a trance-state, all the while rubbing the crystal ball with a soft cloth.

COLOMBINA: Oh goddesses of fate—ye who weave our destinies—send Areo to me. ... Come, Areo, come. ... Ah! I see you—deep in forest mists. Come angel, fly through the mist to me. ... Ah, there you are! Good Areo, in the jumble called humanity, I search for Pompeo of Venice. ... Bring forth Pompeo ... Oh, no! You have got the wrong man. He is wearing a toga. ... Areo, come back! The job is not finished. I did not ask for Pompey—the Roman. I asked for Pompeo of Venice. ... Don't be obstinate! ... Come, whelp, or I shall have Balican whip you. ... That's better. Now, good Areo, lead me to Pompeo of Venice, three years hence. ... Ah! There he is—a clear vision. Three years to the day from now. Well done, imp, well done. ... Pompeo stands like a hero, Beatrice sits aloof, still not committed. ...

What is wrong? ... I can read her heart. She yearns to love Pompeo. Why does she not love him? ... Ah! I see it now: he has failed to woo her.

POMPEO: Woo?

COLOMBINA: Maidens are born with a chill about their hearts. To penetrate that chill a man must woo her, show her that he adores her. He writes a love poem, he delights her with sweet nothings.

POMPEO: I can't write a poem.

COLOMBINA: Think of your love for the girl and practice finding words that rhyme. Inspiration will come to you.

POMPEO: Words that rhyme ... know, go ... friend, bend, send, end. Four words!

COLOMBINA: You see, you can find rhyming words without any trouble. Woo her first to soften her heart. If she is still coy, take her by force. Drag her kicking and screaming until she is on her knees begging you to take her.

POMPEO: Are you sure?

COLOMBINA: I can read her heart. A girl like her secretly longs for a strong man who will take her by force.

POMPEO: That's it! She needs authority. I should have realized that.

COLOMBINA: Remember to woo her first. Don't neglect the poem and the sweet nothings. And be sure to present her with a stunning gift—a sumptuous engagement ring, a ring she will want to show off to all her friends.

POMPEO: I'll start with the poem. Bird, third, wing, sing, love, dove, apple ... All I can think of is grapple—a harsh word. I'll avoid apple.

COLOMBINA: There you are. You will have a poem in no time.

As POMPEO exits, COLOMBINA whacks his rear end with the wand. POMPEO is preoccupied with rhyming words.

POMPEO: Fool, school, gain, pain ... Ouch!

A funeral procession enters. As it crosses the stage men and women bow their heads. COLOMBINA watches the procession. While this is going on BRIGHELLA enters from the rear, filches the gold coins, drops a note on COLOMBINA's table, and scoots off. The funeral procession exits.

COLOMBINA: [Picks up the note] "I heard the whole thing. You are a success. Pilgrims are in town. I am going now to send them to you." Pilgrims—whose coins are copper. I won't need them. [Looks in coin box] My gold coins! Brighella! I'll fix him! He will go to jail for this.

COLOMBINA stomps off.

SCENE NINE

The park. BEATRICE, in a dreamy mood, is seated. LEANDRO enters.

BEATRICE: Leandro, how good to see you. Come, sit beside me. I am not afraid of you.

LEANDRO: [Sits] Why should you be afraid of me?

BEATRICE: When I was sixteen, my sisters and I were taught to hide under our beds when you came into view. But I wasn't afraid. You were fascinating: the masked lover, who came, conquered, then slipped quietly into the night. The gossip now is that Leandro, alias Don Juan, is once again on the loose.

LEANDRO: It is an impostor, not me. I have given all that up for a monk's life.

BEATRICE: From rake to monk! You are a man of extremes, Leandro.

LEANDRO: What about you? If you were sixteen when you hid under your bed, you must be twenty-one by now. I see no wedding ring.

BEATRICE: I am presently at war with my father.

LEANDRO: Who is his choice?

BEATRICE: The richest man in Venice: Pompeo.

LEANDRO: Lord save you!

BEATRICE: Why shouldn't a girl have the right to make her own choice?

LEANDRO: In most cases it would turn out worse than Daddy's choice.

BEATRICE: Not in my case. I am determined to choose my own husband. I am already making a list of possible candidates.

LEANDRO: The young bachelors say that Niccolo is your favorite.

BEATRICE: Niccolo was rebuked by the voice of conscience. He is out of my thoughts. I will be looking for a man of rank, sensible, and, of course, rich. ... Why, Leandro, you would qualify.

LEANDRO: Don't put my name on your list. I am a confirmed bachelor.

BEATRICE: Only dry and dusty men take the bachelor oath. You don't look dry and dusty. Come, let me test your pulse. [Takes LEANDRO's wrist] Oh, my! Vigorous, hot-blooded. Bachelorhood is not for you.

LEANDRO: I had no idea that you were so sensuous. You have a spinster reputation.

BEATRICE: You should put no stock in reputations invented by dull boys and silly girls.. ... Now, I will add Leandro to my list.

LEANDRO: Be sure to keep other options open. I must be on my way. Friends await me.

LEANDRO exits hastily.

BEATRICE: Look at him run. He is afraid—not of me, but himself. His resolve to do without women will not last. His pulse raced when I held his wrist. ... He said that the young bachelors think I favor Niccolo: thus and therefore, he has inquired about me. Leandro, I have found you out.

SCENE TEN

The park. Strollers and gossips. Enter STEFANO and FABRIZIO.

FABRIZIO: Stefano, I do not understand you. You told everyone that you were going to Milano on a diplomatic mission; instead you went to Genoa on a pleasure trip.

STEFANO: The diplomatic mission was a story for my wife.

FABRIZIO: Why Genoa? It is such a long trip, especially for a man with a weak heart. I don't understand it. What can you do in Genoa that you can't do in Venice?

STEFANO: Nothing. It is the *way* things are done that differs. In Genoa, the wine flows more freely, the parties are livelier, the ladies more willing. True, there is a better chance of being stabbed in Genoa, but I am willing to risk it. Life might end at any time: one might as well gamble. My wife is approaching. Say nothing about Genoa.

COUNTESS LUCIA enters

LUCIA: Hello Fabrizio.

FABRIZIO: Lucia! It is a pleasure to see you again.

LUCIA: Such flattery. That can only mean that my husband has been up to some mischief. Come on, Fabrizio, the real story.

FABRIZIO: I am sure Stefano will acquit himself very well. If you will excuse me, I must be on my way.

Exit FABRIZIO

LUCIA: Stefano, a woman's hair is on your collar. It is not mine.

STEFANO: We walk through crowded streets. Hairs are carried on the air.

LUCIA: One, two, three, four, five hairs—all from the same head. You have taken to wearing such strong cologne. Is it to cover up a feminine perfume?

STEFANO: Come, Lucia, you are being much too suspicious. Suspicion is a disease: it can wreck lives. Now tell me, how has your day been?

LUCIA: I have been shopping and visiting the female gossip mills. It is tedious, but it seems to be a childless woman's role in life. The Petrovich woman—she is Bulgarian: she says, "You must never give up. In Bulgaria we average six children. Why? We never give up." I— oh! **[Points to another woman]** Stefano, do you know that woman?

STEFANO: I—ah—don't know her, but I recognize her: Countess Rosaura.

LUCIA: She is wearing my necklace.

STEFANO: That can't be. Your necklace is tucked away in my bank vault.

LUCIA: I would swear it is mine.

STEFANO: It is an imitation—no doubt created by a lesser artist.

LUCIA: Are you sure?

LUCIA approaches ROSAURA

STEFANO: Now Lucia, let's not start an incident. Her husband is a member of the Doge's inner circle. Come, let's go.

Undeterred, LUCIA goes up to ROSAURA and is closely examining the necklace, even to the point of fingering it.

ROSAURA: I beg your pardon, but you are quite cheeky!

LUCIA: Your necklace seems to be an exact copy of mine.

ROSAURA: Of all the nerve! Please go away. ... If you won't go, I will.

ROSAURA turns about, starts to walk off, sees STEFANO

ROSAURA: Stefano, darling! Please save me from this female vampire.

STEFANO's expression is a mix of terror, despair and chagrin. It dawns on ROSAURA that she has blundered. LUCIA is furious. Stage goes dark. Bright lights on three faces. FREEZE. BLACKOUT!

Scene Eleven

The park. Enter a funeral procession. One mourner follows the casket, LUCIA. She lets the audience see her necklace, then resumes an expression of mourning. The funeral procession exits.

Scene Twelve

The park. BEATRICE is seated on a bench. POMPEO enters. He is dressed very fancifully.

POMPEO: Sweet Beatrice, I am glad to see you here. I wish to make up to you, for I have neglected my duty.

BEATRICE: What duty?

POMPEO: A lover's duty, which is to woo his beloved.

BEATRICE: Woo. That is a big word for you.

POMPEO: It is a small word, but it will do.

BEATRICE: What does it mean?

POMPEO: To talk nicely to a lady.

BEATRICE: Or perhaps vainly and in vain.

POMPEO: I am not a vain man, though I have good reason to be one. My head is crammed full of knowledge and wonderful ideas. I live in the best society and frankly, I am the envy of its best people.

BEATRICE: You will, I suppose, marry yourself: your wooing has been very self-centered.

POMPEO: I can give you many advantages, Beatrice. You will be an elegant lady who associates with the best society. Servants will attend you. You will ride in a four-horse carriage. You will glide graciously on Venice's canals in a gondola that is more magnificent than any other in Venice—even the Doge's.

BEATRICE: It sounds like a doll's life.

POMPEO: A doll's life. That's a nice thought. When I find a rhyme for it, I will add it to my poem.

BEATRICE: You have written a poem! I don't believe it.

POMPEO: Oh, but I have written a poem. Proof: I will read it to you.

POMPEO removes sheet of paper from his pocket, kneels before BEATRICE then reads.

Sweet Beatrice, I kneel at your feet,
And offer you gifts, all of them sweet.
I am a humble suitor (though I come in a carriage)
To ask for your hand in blissful marriage.
O say the word—say yes to my appeal,
And I shall consider it a very good deal.

POMPEO: How do you like it?

BEATRICE: Well—it is brief. It is best to be brief. What else is on the wooing program?

POMPEO hands BEATRICE a small box tied with a ribbon.

POMPEO: I have brought you a little present.

BEATRICE: It is very light. [**Looks in box**] There is nothing in it—except for the aroma of a very sweet perfume.

POMPEO: Sweet nothings.

POMPEO removes a ring from his pocket

POMPEO: Now the masterpiece: an engagement ring, an enormous, glittering diamond set in a cluster of rubies. You will be the envy of all women.

BEATRICE: I cannot accept it. I am not disposed to marry you.

POMPEO: After all the time and effort I have expended—not to mention money—to have this exquisite creation made up, you are turning it down!

BEATRICE: I am sorry, Pompeo, but I don't love you.

POMPEO: You must come to love me. Your father commands it. Disobey him and you will spend the rest of your days in a convent.

BEATRICE: I will endure a convent rather than give up my right to find my own love in my own way.

POMPEO: If you go to a convent, society will call me a failure. Beatrice, you are destined to be my bride. It is my masculine right.

POMPEO takes hold of BEATRICE's wrist.

BEATRICE: Let go! You will break my wrist.

POMPEO: You are destined to be my woman: I am taking you with me.

A struggle. BEATRICE gives up.

BEATRICE: Oh, Pompeo, sweet Pompeo, I had no idea you were so commanding. Please let go. How foolish I was not to see your mastery. Come, before you drag me off, let me study your noble profile. Oh, foolish, foolish,

foolish girl that I am, I have not seen the nobility in that brow. Let me admire it.

> POMPEO releases BEATRICE and adopts the posture of a Caesar, surveying a land he has just conquered. BEATRICE winds up and lets fly a powerful slap which strikes POMPEO's cheek. SMACK! POMPEO touches his cheek as if a fly had landed on it; he looks for the fly, then shrugs and resumes his pose. When, a few seconds later—WHAM—the blow is felt, POMPEO's collapse is like a circus performance. BEATRICE exits.

SCENE THIRTEEN

> The park, twilight. BRIGHELLA and the CONSTABLE enter, bound together by police bracelets connected by a chain.

BRIGHELLA: I am not a thief! I am a theatrical promoter.

CONSTABLE: Colombina calls you a thief. She says you stole two gold coins from her.

BRIGHELLA: Those coins are mine, not hers. I am the producer of her show. Box office receipts belong to me. I pay her a salary. ... Is that business about the gold coins the basis of this arrest warrant?

CONSTABLE: She went to court and filed charges. You have tweaked the noses of every class of citizen in this city; it is ironic that one of your commedia associates might put you in jail.

BRIGHELLA: I am more worried about the Doge's men. They have a dragnet out looking for me. This arrest—on a charge from which I can easily clear myself—is a stroke of luck. The trial will drag on for months. By then, the Doge's men will have other problems to deal with.

CONSTABLE: Lady Luck seems always to be on your side. I have wondered, Brighella, about your way of life. Have you given thought to your soul?

BRIGHELLA: My soul will no doubt end up in Hell. I have thought of reforming, but it is too late. When I am in Hell, I will pick the Devil's pocket. In Heaven there are no pockets to pick. No temptation, no fun. My soul—wherever it is—shall relish the sport. [**Looks about**] This is not the way to the magistrate's court. Where are we going?

CONSTABLE: I am commanded to bring you to the Doge's palace.

BRIGHELLA: Are you a decoy—one of the Doge's men?

CONSTABLE: I am a constable, doing his job. Come, it is right around the corner.

CONSTABLE and BRIGHELLA exit.

SCENE FOURTEEN

A room in the DOGE's palace. The DOGE is seated at his desk. Others in the room are: LEANDRO, LUCIA, BRIGHELLA, BEATRICE, POMPEO and FULMINATO. DOGE closes a thick dossier.

DOGE: Brighella, step forward.

BRIGHELLA stands to one side of the Doge's desk.

DOGE: It would seem that you have been chronically in trouble with the law. This is the thickest dossier on an individual I have ever seen. Have you ever gone to jail?

BRIGHELLA: No, your Excellency.

DOGE: How do you account for that?

BRIGHELLA: It is my deal with the Ultimate Power. Hell is my destiny: I get to skip jail.

DOGE: Let's not be frivolous: the charge is serious. Before we bring up the charge against you, I would like to know if you have done anything to benefit society.

BRIGHELLA: I have kept judges, lawyers, policemen and bailiffs employed. As a commedia performer, I have entertained the populace and taught them irreverence. I have provided material for the gossip mills to chew over; as you know, gossip is the lifeblood of a city.

DOGE: Even in the jaws of the lion, you make jests. Fulminato, do you have evidence?

FULMINATO: This cape and outer garments of a nobleman were found in Brighella's house.

DOGE: Are they yours, Leandro?

LEANDRO: Yes, your Excellency, they are mine. He got them from one of my servants. The man confessed, just yesterday, that Brighella bribed him.

FULMINATO: We also found articles of jewelry—valuable stuff, stolen from ladies' boudoirs. We also found this purse.

> **FULMINATO hands purse to DOGE, who examines it.**

DOGE: Where did you get it?

BRIGHELLA: I found it in that little park where lovers meet. Its contents had been removed. I have nothing to do with thieves. I am an artist.

> **DOGE removes note from purse and reads it. Folds note and tucks it into his sleeve.**

152

DOGE: I know the fool who owns the purse. Did you read the note, Brighella?

BRIGHELLA: My father said that reading is the work of the devil.

DOGE: Brighella, you have laughed at the State and made a mockery of justice. Can you name one citizen in Venice who would speak on your behalf—give me reason not to have you hanged?

BRIGHELLA: [Alarmed] Hanged!!

DOGE: Hanged.

BRIGHELLA: Hanged! Your excellency, that is too great an honor to confer upon a rogue who lacks the ambition to commit a great crime. Hanging me would sink Venice's reputation.

DOGE: You have earned enough honors to be hanged twice. But once is enough. Would you answer my question: who will speak on your behalf?

BRIGHELLA: I have friends who will vouch for me, but they are currently out of town.

DOGE: Who are they?

BRIGHELLA: Harlequin, Isabella, Pantalone, Scaramuzzia—

DOGE: Commedia characters. Can you name someone from the larger community?

BRIGHELLA is stumped. LUCIA steps forward.

LUCIA: I will speak on his behalf.

DOGE: Countess Lucia! You surprise me.

LUCIA: I am straight-forward in speaking, your Excellency, as was my father. It is true that there are many incidents in Brighella's dossier: they are not boulders, they are pebbles, pranks, not crimes. Brighella delights in playing jokes on us. His most recent joke—playing the part of Leandro, the lover—was an inspired commedia scenario. He did not invade boudoirs: he was there by invitation. Sex-starved ladies—whose husbands prefer to plow other fields—were happy to have this lover serve them. If he took a souvenir, it was fair compensation for his services. He did no real harm to Leandro, except to add a little spice to his monastic life. When you think about it: the human vanities that Brighella exposes is a service to the community. If people fail to learn his lessons, that is their fault. Brighella is not a criminal. He is a mischief-maker who enlivens our days. What would Venice do without him?

DOGE: Brighella broke the law and must be punished. What punishment do you propose?

LUCIA: As you know, your Excellency, I recently lost my husband—Count Stefano, whose dear heart finally gave out. He cheated on me: still, I loved him. I endured it for years until at last I cheated on him. I don't regret it. A woman is not supposed to admit that she had an affair: society expects that she will be discreet. The discreet life—the cheating life—has become wearisome; I have decided to leave it. I will do something noble: save a life worth saving. ... I propose that Brighella be sentenced to give up his present ways and become a gentleman.

BRIGHELLA: Your Excellency, I protest. To become a gentleman is the equivalent of a death sentence.

DOGE: The rogue rebukes you, Lucia. Do you persist in this mad proposal?

LUCIA: I do.

DOGE: And how is this penalty to be enforced?

LUCIA: Brighella is to be married to me. As wife and jailer, I will assure that he complies with the verdict.

DOGE: [Aghast] Lucia! Am I to believe what I just heard? It is inconceivable that you—who comes from one of Venice's finest families—would marry a rogue. Your family will be shocked.

LUCIA: They need a shock. My family name confers on me a high social status. I can spend hours chatting with Duchess Blabbermouth: vain, talkative, opinionated, nasty-minded, empty-headed. I want to live a real woman's life.

DOGE: What is a real woman's life?

LUCIA: Loving someone and sharing his ordeal. I am tired of being an ornament. For Brighella, the sentence I have proposed is harsh. I will share his hardship. And if I am blessed with children, my woman's life will be richer still.

DOGE: Very well, Lucia, have it your way. ... You are a fortunate man, Brighella: you have a choice of sentences: to be hanged tomorrow morning or marry Countess Lucia and become a gentleman.

> As he weighs the Doge's options, BRIGHELLA mimes various actions, e.g., hand above head tugging at an imaginary hangman's rope about his neck; forced smiles as he engages in inane chatter with various genteel folk, sipping tea, showing patience with a brat he would like to smack, etc. He mimes hanging.

BRIGHELLA: Nasty!—but quick. [Imagined tea cup, mimed chatter in high society] Ho-ho-ho ... That must have been cute ... The tea is wonderful, exotic ... From

Ceylon! No wonder ... lovely child ... **[Despair]** My choices are a quick death or a prolonged dying. ... Your Excellency, is exile an option?

DOGE: No.

LUCIA: Your Excellency, might Brighella and I have a few minutes to parley?

DOGE: Very well, three minutes.

LUCIA takes BRIGHELLA's hand and hauls him to an unoccupied space.

LUCIA: I thought you had a brain. You will not adapt to a genteel society; the society will adapt to you.

BRIGHELLA: Are you in your right mind? I stole your necklace.

LUCIA: If it were something of lesser value, I would have let it go. I had a pleasant hour with you.

BRIGHELLA: I have no aptitude for a gentleman's life. I am a child of the Commedia. I know no other life.

LUCIA: You shall not give up that life. Wear this mask— a sleek, debonair mask, and this cap. There, you look handsome. That is the costume of a renewed Brighella ready to expand his repertoire. You will create a new commedia, one that appeals to the gentry, who can afford higher ticket prices. You will play in theaters and palaces, not platforms erected in a town square. The commedia spirit will be renewed, not lost.

A kiss. BRIGHELLA walks hand-in-hand with LUCIA to the DOGE.

BRIGHELLA   Your Excellency, I accept Countess Lucia's sentence.

DOGE: You will now associate with people you have mocked and robbed; you will treat them honestly and with respect. You will upgrade your wardrobe and your toilette. If you revert to your old ways, the hanging sentence will be carried out.

BRIGHELLA and LUCIA exit.

Scene Fifteen

DOGE: The next item on my agenda concerns you, Beatrice. I have a letter from the Commendatore, your father. He says that he has worked diligently to get you the best possible husband. Instead of being grateful, you are a rebellious girl who defies his wishes. ... Where is your father?

POMPEO: He is not well, your Excellency. He asked me to speak for him.

DOGE: What have you to say to your father's charges, Beatrice?

BEATRICE: I am a loving daughter, dutiful to my father. I do not consider myself to be rebellious. But *my* future happiness is at stake—not Papa's, mine. I believe that I ought to have my own way in the matter of choosing a husband.

DOGE: The laws of Venice are on your father's side.

BEATRICE: If I could choose my husband, I would be the happiest woman in Venice.

DOGE: Your father has chosen Pompeo, who is judged by all to be an excellent man.

BEATRICE: I am sure that Pompeo is an excellent man, but a girl does not fall in love with a quality called excellence.

DOGE: What say you to Pompeo?

BEATRICE: Pompeo, I am afraid that you and I would not make a very good match.

POMPEO: Thank goodness!

DOGE: [**Surprised**] Do you give up your claim, Pompeo?

POMPEO: Yes. I don't want to spend a lifetime dodging the voice of conscience.

DOGE: Suppose, Beatrice, that the laws of Venice were, for a few moments, suspended. Who would you choose for a husband?

BEATRICE: I would choose a man who can command a rebellious girl, a man who could claim her very soul. That man exists. ... His name is Leandro.

LEANDRO: That is very kind of you, Beatrice, but I must remind his Excellency that I have taken a solemn religious oath to live a bachelor's life.

DOGE: Are you referring to the papers you signed when you left the monastery.

LEANDRO: Yes.

DOGE: How carefully did you read them?

LEANDRO: They were in Latin. It was a struggle, but I got through them.

DOGE: I am fluent in Latin: I read them carefully. Your oath is not to live a bachelor's life, but a virtuous life.

LEANDRO: The friars spoke of a bachelor's life as the most virtuous life.

DOGE: For a friar that would certainly be true, but not for a man about town, a man who ought to have heirs, a man suited for advancement in our republic. ... What is your opinion of Beatrice?

LEANDRO: She is a rebellious girl who has caused her father grief. Would she not do the same to her husband? Then, too, there is that dreaded voice of conscience.

BEATRICE: The voice of conscience shall be stilled for my husband. Rebellion will be transformed into its other self: pure love given freely by a generous heart.

DOGE: [Studies Leandro] Leandro, will you take Beatrice for your wife?

LEANDRO: There are days and nights when I miss having a companion—and children's laughter. [Contemplates Beatrice] Look at her: no pleading, a free spirit even in her most desperate moment. ... I will take her.

> BEATRICE takes LEANDRO's hand. They stand side by side, hand in hand.

DOGE: Beatrice and Leandro shall marry. Beatrice, I will send your father word of my decision.

> The Doge slips into an introspective mood.

POMPEO: [Aside, to Leandro] The Commendatore will want to get out of paying the dowry. He pleads poverty, but he has lots of money.

LEANDRO: He will have me and the Doge to deal with if he attempts to evade it. He is a notorious skinflint. I will squeeze him to the limit.

POMPEO: He deserves it.

DOGE: [Speaks his thoughts] Lucia occupies my thoughts. She is headstrong but nonetheless an excellent woman. I respect her decision. I will invite her to be married in my private chapel.

> EXIT ALL

SCENE SIXTEEN

LUCIA, BRIGHELLA, CONSTABLE

CONSTABLE: You filched a duke's purse. That alone would get a man hanged. But luck was with you, Brighella. You escaped the law's vengeance.

BRIGHELLA: Brighella escaped by becoming invisible. He is replaced by a new man: the new Brighella. The old Brighella has vanished from the earth—without ceremony.

LUCIA: The new Brighella will renew the Commedia. And he will be a good father.

BRIGHELLA: A father! Is something cooking?

LUCIA: Yes.

BRIGHELLA: Yet another responsibility. I wonder if I will ever get back on a stage.

LUCIA: Everyone at Lady Lucinda's party loved you. You were the life of the party. Your stories—mimed and spoken—were much more interesting that the commedia's knockabout gags. Their stories, told again and again, have worn thin. After our baby is born, you and I will introduce a new comedy for a new age.

BRIGHELLA: You and me?

LUCIA: I will be the company manager. Someone has to watch the money—and you. The Doge expects it of me. I am your adoring wife and strict but affectionate jailer.

BRIGHELLA: A new comedy for a new age: I like the idea. ... Still, I shall mourn my lost Brighella.

> Funeral procession crosses the stage. LUCIA says a prayer. BRIGHELLA's stoical expression masks his feelings. The procession exits.

CONSTABLE: It is time to end this comedy. The last word goes to you, Brighella. One word that summarizes everything you have learned from this adventure.

BRIGHELLA: One word?

CONSTABLE: You may consult a philosopher's book of words.

> The CONSTABLE sets the book on a stand next to BRIGHELLA, who flips through its pages. His face brightens as he finds a word. He begins to form the word, then stops, frowns, and decides that it won't do. He flips more pages, finds another word, opens his mouth to speak it, and again stops. He shoves the dictionary aside.

BRIGHELLA: These are thought words: they have too many syllables.

> BRIGHELLA simulates the pull of the rope around his neck. LUCIA mimes the act of removing the rope and casting it aside.

BRIGHELLA: What are the chances of a rogue being saved by an aristocrat?

> Again BRIGHELLA simulates the pull of the rope. He realizes how narrow his escape was. He wipes his brow and says—

BRIGHELLA: WHEW!!

BLACKOUT

FINI

FunBirds

A Comedy

CAST OF CHARACTERS

Roger Coyne, Master Architect, age forty-nine
Edna Brophy, Senior Architect, mid-forties
Desiree Duncan, Associate Architect, mid-twenties
CJ Morran,* Chairlady of the Board, age carefully disguised
Amelia, Receptionist, thirty-five (or any older age)
Perry Larsen, Senior Partner, a lawyer, fifty
Lucretia Coyne, Roger's Wife, a lawyer, mid-forties

THE PLACE / THE SETTINGS

The Place: The Theater **

The Setting: The Offices of Morran
& Selby, Architects, Honolulu

SCENE SUMMARY

Prelude: The Theater, the day of the performance
Reality One: Honolulu, an afternoon in January
Interlude: The Theater, the day of the performance
Reality Two: Honolulu, an afternoon in April
Postlude: The Theater, the day of the performance

* Morran rhymes with foreign
** The place is the theater in which the play is being performed

Prelude: The Theater

The characters in the play appear in a space which is light without substance. AMELIA surveys her on-stage colleagues, then addresses the audience.

AMELIA: My opening lines are ridiculous!

EDNA: Stop extemporizing, Amelia. Just speak the speech I gave you.

AMELIA: **[Melodramatic]**

Imagine islands thrust up from the sea
That came to be called Hawaii.
Lush islands under a golden sun,
Spoiled by the human quest for fun.

AMELIA: **[Candid]** Quest for fun. Yuk. Edna, you draw beautifully. Why do you write poems?

EDNA: To set the scene for our audience.

AMELIA: You want this audience to believe that we are in Hawaii. We are obviously not in Hawaii. We are in a building in [City/town in which the theater is located].

EDNA: In a theater you can be anywhere you like. Theater is a place where imagination rules. Now, please go on.

AMELIA: **[To audience]** For us, who are authors of ourselves, this theater is a universe; its places are states of mind. The state of mind in which our story takes place has the name of a real place: Honolulu, Hawaii. But our Honolulu is not a physical place: it is a mood, a style of life. **[Surveys her colleagues]** When you see us—the Honolulu characters—

AMELIA, DESIREE, ROGER, CJ MORRAN and EDNA raise their hands.

AMELIA: —think of palm trees, coconut groves, gorgeous beaches, crystal blue ocean waters—

ROGER: —an island paradise where one lives a life in the sun.

LUCRETIA: There is another state-of-mind in which our story takes place: Chicago, Illinois. When you see us—

LUCRETIA and PERRY raise their hands.

PERRY: Imagine a city of concrete and steel on the edge of a wind-swept northern lake. Our summers are hot, our winters ice cold. But neither heat nor cold keeps us from doing our daily tasks.

AMELIA: We are a group of people who got into a real-life situation that we could not bring to a satisfactory conclusion.

PERRY: A conundrum.

CJ MORRAN: In plain English, a hopeless mess.

AMELIA: We tried to forget it, get on with our lives. But it bugged us. Vanity was at stake: yes, every one of us is vain. Every one of us was convinced that things should have worked out in his or her favor. We had to do something. We consulted a Samoan prophetess, a psychiatrist. Nothing worked. We could not live with ourselves unless we found a solution. But, how was this seemingly impossible task to be done? It was Edna who had the inspiration.

EDNA: We entered the theater. In the theater there is no past, only a present. Every performance is a fresh start.

AMELIA: Our hope is that, if we can play, I should say re-live, our parts—

DESIREE: —again, and again, and again—

AMELIA: —we might achieve a solution.

PERRY: [Dour] Thus far, we have not succeeded.

LUCRETIA: There are too many complications.

DESIREE: Love, chicanery—

EDNA: Rivalries, jealousies—

ROGER: Treachery, duplicity—

LUCRETIA: Changes of heart—

PERRY: —unexpected events. The end result is that we have not accomplished what we set out to do.

AMELIA: Neither have we failed. A curious thing happened. We discovered the true law of the theater: plays are performed on a stage, but the real resolution takes place in the hearts and minds of the audience. If we don't get things resolved, our audiences do it for us.

PERRY: This is crazy! There are as many endings as there are audience members.

ROGER: On the other hand, it is quite exciting to be a character in a drama and have no idea what your ultimate fate will be.

AMELIA: [To colleagues, stern] I remind you that our mission is to resolve it ourselves. [To audience] One day—perhaps this very day—vanity will melt away and every heart's desire will be fulfilled.

CJ MORRAN: Heart's desire! Amelia, you have been reading too many women's romances. The typical heart desires to have its own way. Heart's desire is the very thing that keeps us from arriving at a solution.

AMELIA: Playwrights can unravel complications. **[Studies audience]** I can see that this is an intelligent group of playwrights. **[A handclap, to colleagues]** It is time to get started. Characters, take your places.

> **Characters take their places. ROGER is at center stage, EDNA is to his left, DESIREE to his right. Characters address the audience.**

AMELIA: Our story begins on an afternoon in January, possibly February, but not as late as March. I cannot recall what year it is, but it is prior to the age of the cell phone.

CJ MORRAN: We are in the offices of my firm: Morran and Selby, architects, Honolulu. I am CJ Morran.

ROGER: I am Roger—Roger Coyne. My office is right here.

> **EDNA and DESIREE, when describing their locations, mimic opening and closing a door and pressing an ear to a wall.**

DESIREE: I am Desiree. My office is here—next to Roger's. The wall is thin. You can eavesdrop. A door is here.

EDNA: My office is here. Same arrangement: door, thin wall.

CJ MORRAN: My suite is at the front of the building. I wish you could see it.

AMELIA: Sorry, CJ, but everything has to fit this stage. **[To audience]** When CJ appears, she will be there.

CJ MORRAN: Such impertinence! I remind you, Amelia, that I am Chairlady of the Board. You are the office receptionist. You are at the bottom of the corporate ladder, I am at the top.

AMELIA: When we get to Reality, that is the relationship. In the Theater, I am the boss.

CJ MORRAN: [To audience] This is maddening! To be chairlady of the board and have the receptionist giving you orders is—oh, never mind. I simply wish to point out to you that this space—illuminated by a few meager bulbs—is totally inadequate. When you see me, imagine an office suite with plush carpets, a sixteen-foot leather sofa, a prize-winning tropical terrarium, an enormous window that overlooks the Pacific Ocean—

AMELIA: That's enough. Perry, it is your turn.

PERRY: When you see me you will be in the law offices of Larsen and Clarke, Chicago. I am Perry Larsen.

LUCRETIA: I am Lucretia. I, too, am in Chicago.

AMELIA: Now I summon Dionysus, god of the theater, by whose magic we slip seamlessly from one state of being to another. We will now leave this magical space and enter that all-consuming Present called REALITY. We will know nothing but our moment to moment existence, our own passions, our own desires. We will recall nothing that has taken place in this metaphysical space.

CJ MORRAN: You are fortunate, Amelia. If I remembered your impertinent remarks, the first thing I would do is fire you.

AMELIA: [To colleagues] Goodbye friends. When next we meet we will be employees at the firm Morran and Selby: strangers who happen to know each other.

AMELIA goes to her office space. A flash of light brings about the transition to REALITY.

REALITY: ONE

A bright, sunny day. Roger's office. DESIREE and ROGER are in an embrace. EDNA, in her office, eavesdrops, her ear pressed against the wall that separates her office from Roger's.

DESIREE: [Ardently] Oh Roger, you are Hawaii's one and only aristocrat.

ROGER: I am not an aristocrat. I am simply a person who believes that a human being ought to dress properly.

DESIREE: [Adjusts ROGER'S tie] Your tie is too straight.

ROGER: Desiree, I spent ten minutes getting that tie just right.

DESIREE: Roger, you are now in Hawaii, not Michigan.

ROGER: Illinois. Chicago is in Illinois.

DESIREE: Wherever. The point is that in Hawaii, we are casual about the way we dress.

ROGER: I know. It is paradise's only failing.

DESIREE: If you were born and raised here, you would see it differently.

ROGER: I suppose. But I still believe that there ought to be some sense of style.

DESIREE: [Finishes adjusting tie] I will never change you, but I don't want to. All I want to do is make you a little more dashing. There, it is perfect. I will bet your wife never did this for you.

ROGER: She did—for the first year or two.

DESIREE: You will soon be free of her.

ROGER: I don't know what is happening. It has been three days since I heard from my lawyer. [Checks watch] Our day is slipping away. I have a presentation to rehearse. And surely you have things to do.

DESIREE: Slave driver. [An impulse, lowers voice] Dollars to donuts, Edna is eavesdropping. She always stands in the same spot. [Paces] Right about here ...

> DESIREE has located a spot directly opposite the place where EDNA's ear is pressed to the wall. She picks up a paperweight and is set to throw it at the wall.

ROGER: Desiree!

DESIREE: [Loud enough to be heard] All I want to do is bang a wall.

> EDNA jumps back from the wall.

ROGER: There is work to be done.

> DESIREE thumbs her nose at the wall. EDNA, on the other side of the wall, reciprocates. DESIREE enters her office. ROGER consults his notes as he practices his presentation.

ROGER: Where was I? ... Ah, here we are ... In summary, ladies and gentlemen, the Butler Pavilion—as we have conceived it—is a perfect marriage of man-made structures and the natural setting of Hawaii.

> ROGER pauses to consult his notes. Lights up on LUCRETIA and AMELIA. LUCRETIA is in a separate space.

LUCRETIA: [**On phone**] I would like to speak to Mr. Coyne, please.

AMELIA: I will try, Mrs. Coyne.

Intercom buzzes. ROGER pushes button on intercom.

ROGER: Roger Coyne.

AMELIA: Mr. Coyne, your wife is on the wire.

ROGER: Amelia, what were my instructions?

AMELIA: You are taking no calls from females in Chicago named Lucretia.

ROGER: Correct. Knowing that, why did you bother me?

AMELIA: She is such a lady. I thought maybe you had changed your mind.

ROGER: I have not changed my mind. Tell her I have nothing to say to her. If my lawyer calls, put him through.

AMELIA: Will do.

ROGER clicks off the intercom, then becomes absorbed in his notes.

AMELIA: I am sorry, Mrs. Coyne. I did my best.

LUCRETIA: Thanks for trying, Amelia. Would you give Roger a message from me?

AMELIA: I am ready.

LUCRETIA: [**Dictates**] Roger, I have things to discuss with you. I have called half a dozen times. In every instance, you were in your office, but refused to talk to me. If you persist in this attitude you will talk to me in a courtroom—in Chicago. That conversation will not be pleasant. You have one more chance. You know my number. Call me or await a summons. Signed, Lucretia. ... Have you got it, Amelia?

AMELIA: I've got it. He'll get it.

LUCRETIA: Thanks, Amelia.

Lights on LUCRETIA and AMELIA go down.

ROGER: [Consults notes] Where was I? Ah, yes—the key word is harmony ... [Waves pointer at something on drawing] Shoo—off with you. Shoo.

ROGER examines the drawing, then pushes a button on the intercom. A buzz is heard. EDNA pushes the button on her receiver.

EDNA: Edna Brophy.

ROGER: Edna, I caught your fly.

EDNA: Roger, I don't have a fly.

ROGER: The one you drew on my design for the Butler Pavilion.

EDNA: What makes you suspect me? It might be Desiree's fly—

DESIREE cracks opens the door between hers and Roger's offices and listens.

ROGER: A fly which is so real that I actually tried to shoo it off is yours, Edna—no doubt about that.

EDNA: I would suggest that you leave it there. Whoever heard of a tropical setting without a bug?

ROGER: It is a good thing I noticed it. If CJ were to see it, she would fire you.

EDNA: CJ has fired me half a dozen times, but I am still here. I am a survivor, you can't get rid of me. I have brewed chamomile tea. Would you like a cup?

ROGER: No thanks. I have to eradicate a bug.

DESIREE: [**Pokes head through door**] Roger, I want you to know that I would never put a fly on your drawing.

EDNA: [**At her door**] She would have drawn a tarantula— a crawling, grasping, poisonous—

DESIREE: Eradicate that fly, Roger, before it gives you the purple plague.

ROGER: Ladies! I believe we all have work to do.

> **DESIREE slams her door, EDNA slams her door. ROGER resumes his bug-eradication project. Lights up on AMELIA and PERRY .**

PERRY: [**On phone**] Is Mr. Coyne there?

AMELIA: I will put you through, Mr. Larsen.

> **Phone rings. ROGER picks it up. Light on AMELIA goes down.**

ROGER: Roger Coyne.

PERRY: It is me, Perry.

ROGER: Where have you been?

PERRY: My building has been closed for two days. We have had a blizzard—twenty-six inches!

ROGER: Whoosh! What is the temperature like?

PERRY: With the wind chill, minus twenty. Telephone lines are down, pipes are frozen all over town.

ROGER: I am glad I left that behind.

PERRY: C'mon, Roger—an old Chicagoan like you—I'll bet you miss it.

ROGER: Not a bit. I am living a life in the sun and enjoying every minute of it. Last night, while you were freezing in Chicago, Edna and I strolled on Makaha beach and watched the sun set over the Pacific.

PERRY: Edna. Is she the young one or the old one?

ROGER: The word is mature. She is mature, sensible, has a wonderful sense of humor. She is talented, too. She draws illustrations for nature books. She writes poetry and plays. A little theater did a play of hers just recently.

PERRY: She sounds like a nice person. What has Lucretia concerned is that you are dating a girl young enough to be your daughter.

ROGER: I was not aware that you have been so chummy with Lucretia. She is our adversary.

PERRY: I meet her periodically—during arbitration conferences. She tells me what she thinks of your new life. I can't prevent her from doing that.

ROGER: You can tell her to mind her own goddam business. ... Is Hapless still her lawyer?

PERRY: Hapley. Buzz Hapley. Yes, he is her lawyer.

ROGER: Is she still working for him?

PERRY: Yes. He says she is helluva good trial lawyer.

ROGER: How is the romance between them going?

PERRY: All right, I suppose. Hapley is hard to read. But you didn't answer my question. Is it true—what Lucretia says about the young one?

ROGER: The young lady's name is Desiree. She *is* young enough to be my daughter, but she is not my daughter.

PERRY: Dez-ee-ray—?

ROGER: As in desire!

PERRY: [**Eyebrows raised**] Desire—

ROGER: You've got it, Perry old man—you have got it. Desiree. You don't pronounce the name, you let it roll off your tongue.

PERRY: Roger, you surprise me!

ROGER: Perry, your prudishness is showing.

PERRY: I am not being prudish. What I am talking about is common sense. You are a man of distinction, people look up to you. Your children look up to you. To hear you talking about a lascivious-sounding name rolling off your tongue is—well, it is not common sense.

ROGER: Your common sense applies to Chicago, where life is all squares and rectangles and gears that have to mesh. I have moved to a place where the contours of life are soft. I have discovered the new art of living: I do what *I* want to do. There are two women in my life—why not? Desiree is young, vivacious, endless fun. Edna is fun in a mature way. When I am in the mood for a quiet evening—a classical concert, a stroll on the beach at sunset, Edna is the perfect partner. I do the fling things with Desiree: dances, beach parties, sailing, surfing. I even surf, Perry—can you believe that?

PERRY: Roger, this life of yours sounds idyllic. But, if I may raise a practical issue, how do your two ladies like this arrangement? Do they get along with each other?

ROGER: [**Lowers his voice**] Well, no, they don't get along.

PERRY: That doesn't surprise me. No woman—married or unmarried—is willing to share her man with another woman. It is a fact of life. You cannot change it.

ROGER: The world has changed, Perry. Women have been liberated—men, too. People don't marry, they live together. Relations are informal.

PERRY: Roger, Hawaii has changed you, and I am not sure I like what I am hearing. An excess of anything—especially sunshine—is not good for a man.

ROGER: An excess of blizzards is worse. But never mind that: how is the divorce coming along?

PERRY: [A sigh] Not good. Lucretia is making new demands.

ROGER: Perry, I thought we had a deal worked out. Lucretia agreed to it, Buzz Hapless thought it was fair to everyone. All that remained was for you and Hapless—

PERRY: Hapley—

ROGER: Hapley. You and he were to iron out a few details and finalize the divorce.

PERRY: Lucretia is getting sticky about the details. Roger, she is serious. She will not agree to a thing until you come to Chicago. She has some things to say to you.

ROGER: Lucretia wants me to go to Chicago?

PERRY: It might be a good idea. If you were to come here and see her—you know, talk things over ...

ROGER: I know she wants to talk to me, but I have nothing to say to her. What is it, Perry? Don't tell me it's for old time's sake. What is the real reason. Is she having second thoughts about life with Hapless?

PERRY: Hapley.

ROGER: Hapley. What does she want to talk about?

PERRY: You. When she heard about this new life of yours—with two women you call FunBirds, she positively bristled.

ROGER: You remind her, Perry, that it was she who walked out on me. She wanted the divorce. I have started a new life. I will do it my way. I expect her to live up to the agreement we had before I left.

PERRY: I will do my best.

ROGER: Do that. Good bye.

> ROGER slams the phone on to the receiver. PERRY's office fades to black. ROGER sits at the telephone table, stewing. Lights up on CJ MORRAN. Intercom buzzes. DESIREE answers.

DESIREE: This is Desiree.

CJ MORRAN: Dugan! This is CJ Morran.

DESIREE: The name is Duncan—Desiree Duncan.

CJ MORRAN: Oh yes, Duncan.

DESIREE: Your fifth husband was named Dugan.

CJ MORRAN: Ah, yes—Dugan. He had a magnificent chin. I had a weakness for chins in those days. But never mind that. Dugan, be a good girl and bring me the drawings for the Hanes Annex.

> CJ clicks off. DESIREE extracts a rolled up drawing from a pigeon hole in a cabinet beneath her drafting table.

DESIREE: [Mimics CJ] Doo-gan, be a good girl and bring me the drawings for the Hanes Annex. [Opens door

to Roger's office] Roger, her highness has summoned me. She wants the drawings for the Hanes Annex. We are adding six stalls to the ladies room—she calls that an annex.

ROGER: Good luck, darling.

As DESIREE exits through a door at the rear of her office. CJ attacks another button on her intercom. Intercom buzzes. EDNA answers.

EDNA: This is Miss—

CJ MORRAN: Brody! This is CJ Morran.

EDNA: Brophy—the name is Brophy.

CJ MORRAN: Oh, yes—Brophy—

EDNA: Brody was your third husband.

CJ MORRAN: The third? Let's see ... Hefner, Fletcher, then came—Brody—yes, you are right! Now, Brody—

EDNA: Brophy—

CJ MORRAN: Really Brophy, you ought to change your name. Change it to Dowd. No—come to think of it, I once had a husband named Dodd. If you were Dowd, I would call you Dodd. But never mind that, I have a note to call you.

EDNA: I did not leave a message.

CJ MORRAN: Who did?

EDNA: I don't know, but I can guess. It is a young woman who mimics me and you.

CJ MORRAN: Mimics me! Who is it?

EDNA: I don't want to say a name until I have proof.

CJ MORRAN: Get the proof, then call me. I will not tolerate office pranksters having jokes at my expense.

EDNA: I will do what I can.

> **EDNA signs off. CJ attacks another button. Intercom buzzes. ROGER answers.**

ROGER: Roger Coyne.

CJ MORRAN: [Cooing] Roger, darling—

> **EDNA eavesdrops.**

ROGER: CJ! And how is my favorite chairlady of the board today?

CJ MORRAN: All aflutter, Roger—all aflutter. The decision is due on the Hammaker Building. If we get it, it will be the biggest deal we have ever had. I have heard via the grapevine that their selection committee is absolutely ecstatic over your design.

ROGER: I am confident, CJ—but I don't believe in putting all our eggs in one basket. Get on with the next project. Wait till you see it—the Butler Pavilion. It's all ready. Hang on, CJ—I'll push a few buttons and the drawings will be printed in your office. [Pushes computer buttons] There we are—it is done.

CJ MORRAN: Roger, you have infused new life into this firm. ... There has been a vacant partnership since Mr. Selby left us—

ROGER: Your former husband—

EDNA: [Ear pressed against wall] Oh-oh!

CJ MORRAN: Mr. Selby was more of a tax write-off than a husband.

ROGER: All your partners have been husbands ...

CJ MORRAN: One has to think of the tax advantages.

ROGER: You have had seven partners—

CJ MORRAN: —and exactly the same number of husbands. But never, Roger, have I encountered a man of your genius. Think of the possibilities: we could be Morran and Coyne. All it takes is a little paint on the door.

ROGER: And, I suppose, a marriage license.

CJ MORRAN: Roger, dearest, is that a proposal?

ROGER: I cannot make any proposals. I have a wife in Chicago.

CJ MORRAN: Good heavens! Aren't you divorced yet?

ROGER: It takes time, CJ, it takes time.

CJ MORRAN: You people from the Midwest take this sort of thing much too seriously.

ROGER: It is still my first year in Hawaii. It takes a while to get rid of old habits.

CJ MORRAN: Well, get on with it, Roger, do get on with it. And good luck with the Hammaker building.

ROGER: Thanks, dear.

> **ROGER signs off. CJ'S office fades to black. ROGER resumes his fly eradication project. Lights up on AMELIA. Intercom buzzes. ROGER answers it.**

ROGER: Roger Coyne.

AMELIA: Mr. Coyne, there is a gentleman on the phone. He says he is from some kingdom.

ROGER: Kingdom—? Is he one of those Jehovah people?

AMELIA: He has an oriental accent.

ROGER: Oh— Oh, yes—put him through, Amelia—put him through.

> AMELIA makes the connection but continues to listen. ROGER picks up the phone. EDNA, who is intensely curious, cracks open the door between her office and Roger's, and listens.

ROGER: Hello. ... Mister Iosso, how are you? [**Lowers voice**] You have news for me? [**Listens intently**] Just a minute. Amelia, you can sign off now.

AMELIA: Yes, Mr. Coyne, I was just about to do that.

> AMELIA disconnects. Her space fades to black.

ROGER: [**Secretive**] I am sorry, Mister Iosso. You were saying—? [**Listens**] You have something for me ... The location we discussed—perfect! How soon? ... You will call. I look forward to it. ... Bye.

> ROGER hangs up the phone, goes to the globe, twirls it about, then studies it with a magnifying glass. EDNA affects a casual entry.

EDNA: Are you thinking of taking a trip?

ROGER: Oh—I was daydreaming ...

EDNA: [**Looks at globe**] Over the middle of the Pacific Ocean—?

ROGER: Yes, it is deep and unfathomable.

EDNA: I see. [**Adjusts ROGER's tie**] Your tie is crooked.

ROGER: What is it that prompts women to rearrange my tie?

EDNA: I am doing it because Desiree made a mess of it. There—it is just right.

ROGER: Are you sure?

EDNA: I have never known a man who dresses as meticulously as you do.

ROGER: One should dress well.

EDNA: I am following your example. How do like my new dress?

ROGER: [His mind elsewhere] She is out of her mind!

EDNA: Who?

ROGER: Lucretia—thinking she can get me to go to Chicago.

EDNA: You did not answer my question. I asked you if—

ROGER: I know what you asked. [Ardent, looks deep into EDNA's eyes] And my answer is: yes, your dress is beautiful. And you are more than beautiful: you are exquisite.

EDNA: Oh, Roger, darling. I do it for you.

An embrace, a kiss

ROGER: You are everything to me, Edna, the sun, the moon, the stars in the skies.

EDNA: Oh, Roger, you are the fire that gives me life. I love you.

An embrace, a kiss. EDNA fusses with ROGER's tie.

EDNA: Roger, if you should decide to go back to Chicago—I mean, if it were necessary—I would go with you. I would stand by you. I would not leave you to face Lucretia alone.

ROGER: [**Startled, annoyed**] What makes you think that I am afraid to face Lucretia?

EDNA: You refuse to take her phone calls. You won't talk to her—confront her.

ROGER: Why should I? I have nothing to say to her. Afraid? That is absurd! I am not going to Chicago. And you should not even think of going there. You are the antidote to Chicago.

EDNA: [**Without enthusiasm**] I am delighted to hear it.

ROGER: Edna, you are everything a modern woman ought to be: you have developed your talents, you have maintained your career.

EDNA: I suppose.

ROGER: It is essential to your freedom—your autonomy.

EDNA: Roger, I would prefer that you look at me in a more realistic way. I make my living doing routine architectural work. It is very professional, but dull. The things I enjoy doing are not taken seriously. The bugs I draw are not used in bug books: they are used in bird books; my birds are in bug books. I am a writer. My poems are read by eight other poets. I write plays in verse that no one takes seriously.

ROGER: I take it seriously. How many people can say that they had a play performed in a theater?

EDNA: It was not a performance, it was a staged reading—five readings to steadily diminishing audiences. The only audience for the fourth reading was you and me. Not even I attended the last one. By the way, you never did tell me what you thought of it.

ROGER: I loved it!

EDNA: Roger, I sat next to you. I can distinguish between profound concentration and dozing.

ROGER: The Polynesian symbolism was a little
hard to follow, but the ecological disaster at the end
was—ah—devastating!

> **DESIREE** reenters her office via the rear door.
> **Eavesdrops.**

EDNA: [**Agitated**] I am the last American to write plays in
verse. No one will succeed me. It won't matter. Nothing
matters. Architecture doesn't matter, bugs and birds don't
matter, poetic drama doesn't matter.

ROGER: Edna, you are talking nonsense. You do interesting things, you have a wonderful life.

EDNA: It is a clever life, but it lacks commitment. I am
ready for a change. A while ago you were staring dream-
like at the Pacific Ocean. What was that about?

ROGER: What would you think of living on a south seas
island?

EDNA: That sounds fascinating!

> **Roger is Astonished at the intensity of EDNA's**
> **response.**

ROGER: You would go with me?

EDNA: Oh, darling, yes, yes, yes. I want to do something
new with my life, something creative. I want to roll the
dice—with you, no one but you.

ROGER: Edna, you are mad, but I love you for it.

ROGER and EDNA embrace. DESIREE cracks the door open, peeks into Roger's office, then closes the door.

DESIREE: This is getting out of hand! ... What to do ... to do ... to do ... to do ...

An idea, mimics CJ Morran

DESIREE: Brody ... Bro-o-dee ...

EDNA and ROGER disengage. He gazes into her eyes, an ardent tone.

ROGER: Edna, darling, you are divine ...

DESIREE pushes the intercom button. It buzzes in Roger's office. ROGER pushes a button on the intercom.

ROGER: Roger Coyne—

DESIREE: Roger, this is CJ. Is Brody in your office?

EDNA: This is Edna Brophy.

DESIREE: Brody, I am at this moment looking at your plan for the renovation of the cafeteria in the Homer P. Smith School. The plumbing is UPSIDE DOWN. Come to my office immediately and explain it.

DESIREE clicks off the intercom.

EDNA: Upside down—? What on earth is that woman talking about? I will be back, Roger.

EDNA leaves. DESIREE enters Roger's office.

DESIREE: [A buss] Darling. [Adjusts tie] Your tie is all wrong. Roger, when are you going to disillusion Edna?

The poor woman thinks you are in love with her. You should tell her, Roger. If you don't, you might have a suicide on your hands.

ROGER: Desiree, using CJ Morran for your practical jokes will one day cost you your job.

DESIREE: What makes you suspect me?

ROGER: I have never heard of upside down plumbing.

DESIREE: All right, next time I will say something about the decor. Edna uses too much yellow.

ROGER: You silly twit, there won't be a next time. When Edna marches into CJ's office and finds that CJ had not called her at all, she will be on to the trick and you won't fool her again.

DESIREE: Roger—do you really think I am too young for you?

ROGER: Whatever put that idea into your head?

DESIREE: You refer to me as a twit.

ROGER: A figure of speech—

DESIREE: Sometimes I have the feeling that you think of me as a plaything. You never talk to me about serious things. I know for a fact that you talk about the serious matters in your life with Edna, but not with me.

ROGER: What serious matters?

DESIREE: Your past life, what your kids are like. You have never said so much as a word to me about your marriage or Buzz Hopeless.

ROGER: Hapless.

DESIREE: Whatever. You never discuss these issues with me.

ROGER: Let's not talk about it.

DESIREE: You see, you are proving my point.

ROGER: With you, darling, I have fun. I leave the wreckage of the past behind me.

DESIREE: Roger, I do not know what you see in Edna— or for that matter, CJ Morran.

ROGER: What makes you think I see anything in CJ?

DESIREE: I had to bring the Hanes drawings to her— remember? When I arrived at her office, she was on the intercom with dearest Roger, dangling a partnership in front of his nose. Her war paint was positively aglow.

ROGER: Really?

DESIREE: CJ does not offer partnerships to men who have not given her at least a little encouragement.

ROGER: I have not given her encouragement, and I don't need a partnership. I take no salary. I get a percentage of all my designs which sell.

DESIREE: You do? I will bet you have told Edna that; you have never once mentioned it to me.

ROGER: With you, my love, all things mundane are forgotten.

DESIREE: Well, I want to talk about it.

ROGER: What?

DESIREE: Your percentage deal.

ROGER: All right. What do you want to know?

DESIREE: Ah—well—how much?

ROGER: Fifty percent.

DESIREE: Fifty! Roger, how did you get a tightwad like CJ to agree to a deal like that?

ROGER: CJ knew what I could offer the firm. I have designed some of the most prestigious buildings in Chicago. Several of my designs have been featured in national magazines. There was a TV show about me.

DESIREE: Oh Roger, only an aristocrat could do what you have done. You are an absolute aristocrat. I love you for it. I wish you would love me in return.

ROGER: I do love you—

DESIREE: —every other day.

Ardent, ROGER gazes into DESIREE's eyes.

ROGER: If I were to see you every day, I would be a burden. I want to miss you so that I yearn to gaze into your eyes again. Every time I see you I want to fall in love all over again.

DESIREE: Oh Roger!

A kiss

ROGER: Desiree, darling, may I have the pleasure of your company this evening?

DESIREE: Oh my dearest, yes, yes, yes.

ROGER: Tom Cardew is hosting a big bash on the beach.

DESIREE: Are you going to wear slacks, like you did to the last beach party?

ROGER: Of course.

DESIREE: Roger, in Hawaii it is unheard of to wear slacks to a beach party.

ROGER: Except when I am in the ocean, I refuse to be seen in shorts! For a mature man to expose his legs in public is—well, it is not in good taste. [Suddenly doubtful] I suppose the young people laugh at me.

DESIREE: They don't. An aristocrat is entitled to wear slacks to a beach party. You are the only aristocrat in Hawaii. My girlfriends are horribly jealous. Kiss me, darling—

EDNA barges in.

EDNA: That woman is impossible! I walk into her office and there on her desk is my design for the cafeteria in the Homer P. Smith School. You won't believe this, but she said the plumbing was upside down.

ROGER glances at DESIREE, who is exultant.

EDNA: She had the whole drawing upside down! She is too vain to put on her glasses! [Adjusts tie] Roger, your tie is crooked.

DESIREE: [Readjusts tie] Roger, your tie is too straight. It needs a little wave.

EDNA: [Readjusts tie] Crooked is not a wave—it is crooked.

DESIREE: [Readjusts tie] Straight is square.

EDNA: [Readjusts tie] Crooked is juvenile—

DESIREE: [Readjusts tie] Wouldn't some older people love to be juvenile again.

ROGER: [Choking] Ladies—

EDNA: [**Readjusts tie**] One must outgrow juvenile fantasies at some point in life.

DESIREE: [**Readjusts tie**] What do you do when you are with Edna—play croquet?

EDNA: [**Readjusts tie**] With her I suppose you have advanced to the merry-go-round.

ROGER: Enough! I have had enough of this bickering!

EDNA: And I have had enough of this situation!

DESIREE: So have I.

EDNA: This FunBirds business cannot go on. You have got to make up your mind.

ROGER: I can't make up my mind.

DESIREE: That is ridiculous! If your love for her is equal to your love for me, my charms must not impress you.

EDNA: When you compare me to her, I am reduced to a common flirt.

DESIREE: Hah!

EDNA: Just a minute, Desiree—we can have it out later. I want to hear what Roger has to say.

DESIREE: You are right, Edna. Roger, in your heart of hearts you prefer one of us. Who is it?

ROGER: I have searched my heart many times. I have found no answer.

DESIREE: In that case, another method must be found. [**Produces a coin**] Here is a silver dollar. Flip it. Heads, it's Edna, tails, it is me.

ROGER: [**Takes coin**] Well, if you both insist, I—

EDNA: No—wait.

DESIREE: You see, Roger, in her soul of souls she knows that you and I are destined for each other.

EDNA: It isn't that. I don't think this kind of decision lends itself to the coin-toss process.

DESIREE: Then how should he do it?

EDNA: The measure of a man's love is in his words.

DESIREE: Why, Edna, that's a good idea. Roger, tell each of us in turn how much you love us. We will judge which statement is most sincere. Start with Edna. Tell her in your own heart-felt words how much you love her.

ROGER: Here and now? In the presence of both of you? I can't do that.

DESIREE: Come, Roger, tell dear Edna how much you love her. I won't mind hearing it.

ROGER: A man can't just pour his heart out to a crowd.

DESIREE: You see, Edna, he does not love you.

ROGER: Dammit, Desiree, that is not true! If I were without Edna, I would go out of my mind! You have no idea how happy she makes me. If I could not have her in my life, I would swim off into the Pacific Ocean—and I would keep swimming until the sharks took me.

EDNA: Oh, Roger! You see, Desiree, you are an infatuation.

ROGER: How can you say that, Edna? How can you even think it? Desiree is my treasure. If I could not have her in my life, I would go to Paris, France and jump off the Eiffel Tower.

DESIREE: Oh, Roger! Imagine—jumping off the Eiffel Tower—for me! [To EDNA] That is more significant than a swim in the ocean.

EDNA: What do you mean, a swim in the ocean? He would allow sharks to devour him.

DESIREE: A grubby little private suicide. Jumping off the Eiffel Tower makes a statement to the world: I loved and lost Desiree.

Lights up on CJ MORRAN

EDNA: [To Desiree] Stop! Don't say another word. I refuse to go on with this looney game. We ask for sincere words, and we get suicidal statements that are weighted one against the other. It is another evasion—another escape hatch.

Intercom buzzes

ROGER: Roger Coyne.

CJ MORRAN: Roger, darling, you have done it! The Hammaker building is yours, a partnership is yours—if you have sense enough to take it.

ROGER: The Hammaker people—they have accepted my design?

CJ MORRAN: You have earned a handsome commission. What are you going to do with it?

ROGER: It will be the down payment on my very own paradise.

CJ MORRAN: What a mad, impetuous notion! Come to my office right away. A champagne celebration awaits you.

ROGER: Coming, CJ—I am coming. [Hands coin to DESIREE] The Empress beckons. See you later, dears.

ROGER exits. Lights on CJ MORRAN go down.

DESIREE: He always finds an escape hatch!

EDNA: It is his most disagreeable trait. ... Are you satisfied with this situation?

DESIREE: [**Subdued**] No.

EDNA: Neither am I.

DESIREE: Do you have any suggestions?

EDNA: Yes, but you would not want to hear them.

DESIREE: Edna, Roger dates you out of pity. He refers to you as "my poor spinster."

EDNA: And you as "my playmate." Let's be realistic. He dates me for my mind and you for your—personality. Between us, we constitute the ideal woman. He has no incentive to choose between us.

DESIREE: It is worse than that. If things go on as they are now, we will both lose him.

EDNA: Yes, we will both lose him. [**Studies DESIREE**] Well—what is to be done?

DESIREE: It is simple, it is inevitable: one of us has to drop out.

EDNA: Yes—one of us has to drop out. But neither of us will do it.

DESIREE: We could toss a coin.

EDNA: Do you settle everything with a coin toss?

DESIREE: A coin settles a dispute between two girls. [**Produces three dice**] Three dice settles a three-way dispute. If there are more than three, it probably can't be settled.

EDNA: [**Examines coin**] I suppose I might as well rely on a coin. Roger's last name is Coyne. Shall we call it "The Great Coyne Toss."

EDNA hands the coin back to DESIREE who flips it.

DESIREE: Call.

EDNA: Heads.

The coin falls to the floor.

DESIREE: You win.

EDNA: Are you dropping out?

DESIREE: No.

EDNA: I didn't think you would. But I wouldn't have either.

A pause. EDNA and DESIREE study each other.

EDNA: Don't you find this FunBirds business demeaning?

DESIREE: Yes, but it is your fault. You, you—if it were not for you—

EDNA: —you would have Roger to yourself. I do exactly the same thing. I blame you, not Roger.

DESIREE: Do you feel the situation is demeaning?

EDNA: Frankly, yes. I am old fashioned enough to think that men and women ought to make commitments to each other. You know, till death do us part, in sickness and in health—that sort of thing.

DESIREE: Why don't you walk out on him?

EDNA: And turn him over to you—

Pause. Calms herself

EDNA: Put yourself in my position. Where love is concerned, I have had a luckless life. Married at age twenty—a dreadful experience, a year later divorced. Since then, I have had two opportunities, but was afraid to take the plunge. Then—with dread fifty on the horizon—I thought the fates were being kind to me: they brought a man into my life who I could come to love. But then the fates showed that they were making sport with me: they introduced him to a young seductress.

DESIREE: Being young does not make life easy. Young men my age are juveniles. Roger is so sophisticated, so wise, yet lots of fun. When I am with him, life has meaning—real meaning.

EDNA: For you it has meaning. For Roger it has meaning every other day.

DESIREE: I know. But when he holds me in his arms, all doubts vanish.

EDNA: Ditto. ... Would you answer a question? Does he look deep into your eyes, tell you he loves you—and have you feeling that you are the only woman in the world?

DESIREE: Yes ...

EDNA: Me, too. Roger can make me feel that I am the most perfect woman in the world. And when he does that, he is quite sincere.

DESIREE: I feel the same way. But if we both feel that way, how sincere can he be?

EDNA: I have had a sense about Roger. This little conversation is confirming it. He is an actor. He plays two characters, both named Roger Coyne. One Roger performs for you; the other for me.

DESIREE: An actor? There is more to him than that—there must be.

EDNA: He is an actor. How do I know it? It is simple. When I am with him, I am not myself—my true self. I am an actress. I am at times the adoring woman, at other times the chastising woman, or the moody woman, or the happy woman. It is always some variant of the woman. ... How about you?

DESIREE: I put on airs. I play the part of the star-struck girl, or sometimes the petulant girl, then the cheerful girl, then the pouting girl. Actually, I enjoy it. But I must admit that it is growing tiresome. ... I will ask the question I asked before: why haven't you walked out on him?

EDNA: Why? I will tell you why. I have a feeling that one day Roger will gaze into my eyes and come to his senses. And when he does, I will be the only woman in the world, and he will be the best of men. If I am not mistaken, you have the same notion. My problem—and yours—is that he might not get around to it.

DESIREE: We will both lose him. He will fall into another woman's arms.

EDNA: Exactly. There is an old saying: the best way to catch a man is on a rebound. **[Paces, thinks]** I would rather have a fifty-fifty chance than none. ... What is the situation? ... Roger is not only an actor, he is a playwright: the author of an ongoing comedy called FunBirds. ... Roger's comedy has to end.

DESIREE: That is easier said than done.

EDNA: There must be a way. [**Paces**] Think, Edna, think ... I have it! We are already actresses—playing roles in FunBirds. Roger is the author: he writes the script. Why don't we become playwrights? Let's make Roger an actor in our comedy.

DESIREE: It won't work. We don't like each other.

EDNA: Have you ever seen two actresses who detest each other in life, love each other on stage?

DESIREE: The names they love are stage names.

EDNA: That is a convenient arrangement, but not essential. I will play a character named Edna Brophy; you will play a character named Desiree Duncan. What do you think?

DESIREE: Actresses need a plot.

EDNA: Yes, a playwright's plot.

DESIREE: I saw that play of yours, Edna.

EDNA: [**Astonished**] You did?

DESIREE: I went to the last performance. I was the only one in the audience. I wanted to see if you could devise a plot. You didn't.

EDNA: I have learned a few things since I wrote that play.

DESIREE: Oh?

EDNA: I have learned not to invent a plot, but rather to borrow one. Do you know Shakespeare's *Taming of the Shrew?*

DESIREE: That's the wrong plot, Edna. That one is about how men keep women under their thumbs.

EDNA: It is a perfect plot. What we have to do is reverse the sex roles. [**Pacing**] In *Taming of the Shrew*, Petruchio tames the fiery Kate by playing her game—to the hilt. We will do that to Roger. Let's see—our script will be called—what?

DESIREE: You call Roger an actor; my word is rogue.

EDNA: Good. Our title will be *The Taming of Roger Rogue*. This should be fun. [**Paces, talks**] Now here's the plot. Roger, the author of a long-running comedy called *FunBirds* will be our central character. We—the characters called Edna and Desiree—will play Roger's game. Let's accept the fact that we are two women sharing one man.

DESIREE: That is playing right into his hands!

EDNA: The idea of having everything you ever wanted is a fantasy. What we have to do is make it real. That's what Petruchio did to Kate. ... I feel a mood coming on—a malicious one—an urge to teach Roger Rogue a lesson. Will you join me?

DESIREE: Yes—I will do it! [**Sudden despair**] No, I won't. It won't work! We don't like each other.

EDNA: It will work if we can stop being ourselves. If we become the actresses playing ourselves, we will succeed. The big step is to get into our roles. Are you ready?

> **DESIREE nods a circumspect 'yes'. EDNA takes a few seconds to adopt the posture and tone of an actress in a high comedy.**

EDNA I'll start with my line.

> **An utterly fraudulent smile**

EDNA: Desiree, darling, shall we cooperate in a plot to kill Roger—with kindness, of course? Shall we be the best of friends?

DESIREE: Edna, darling, I—I can't say it. I gag on the best-of-friends part.

EDNA: Think of something you would like to say about me.

DESIREE: That's easy.

EDNA: Now smile. [Desiree smiles] That's it. Now, don't say those nasty words that came to mind; instead keep the feeling and speak the words I gave you. Come now, you can do it. The first two words are 'Edna, darling.'

DESIREE: [The actress] Edna, darling, I'd love to co-operate with you in a plot to tame our favorite rogue— [Breaks off] I can't say the best-of-friends part.

EDNA: [Quick, intense] Envision Roger—at this very moment—in CJ Morran's arms.

DESIREE: He wouldn't—

EDNA: Oh yes, he would. She has offered him a part-nership. They have had a glass of champagne; then—in a giddy mood—a second glass. And now, as they inch their way toward the sixteen-foot leather sofa—

DESIREE: Stop it!

EDNA: Aah! You do love him, don't you?

DESIREE: And you do not. Otherwise you could not describe that scene so coldly.

EDNA: I love Roger as much as you do. But the thought of him being in another woman's arms no longer makes me angry. I am beyond anger. I am cool, calculating, vindictive. I am even willing to enter into a bargain with the woman who I— [A wicked smile]—have decided to admire.

> DESIREE studies her a moment, then breaks into a smile that matches that of EDNA—indeed exceeds it in vindictiveness.

DESIREE: [The actress] The taming of Roger Rogue! Edna, dearest, what a marvelous idea! And, of course, we shall be the best of friends. We shall be more than friends, we shall be sisters.

EDNA: Desiree—dearest—I knew you could do it.

DESIREE: [Herself] That image of Roger in CJ's arms did it. I suddenly realized that—if it were to his advantage—he would do exactly that. How shall we tame him?

EDNA: We will agree to his terms. We will inform him jointly that we have agreed to share him.

DESIREE: Isn't there a better way?

EDNA: Nothing I know of beats Petruchio's way. He was Shakespeare's greatest hero. None of the others could have tamed the fiery Kate. When I was seventeen I was madly in love with Petruchio. I would have followed him to the ends of the earth; I would have borne him seventeen children. When I was seventeen I was a mad romantic; today I am a female desperado.

DESIREE: Edna, this is the twentieth century. Do you really think we can do unto Roger what Petruchio done unto to Kate?

EDNA: Yes—if we study Petruchio, learn from him. He anticipated Kate's every want, every whim. He killed her with kindness. We shall do that to Roger.

DESIREE: I get it. We will anticipate Roger's every whim. In return, he must allow us our woman's whims. I shall want to do something special every night that he is mine. I will keep him up until the wee hours of the morning.

EDNA: I will do the same. Night after night he goes without sleep.

DESIREE: And, since there are two of us, we get a night's sleep every other night.

EDNA: We will always be cheerful, happy, thrilled to be able to share him.

DESIREE: [**The actress**] It will be a pleasure to kill Roger with kindness—mean-spirited, overbearing kindness. [**Herself**] It is hard to believe I said that—yet I meant it. That malicious imp of yours has got hold of me too. ... Poor Roger, I do love him.

EDNA: So do I. But we must not allow ourselves to feel sorry for him. Remember—one of us will lose everything.

EDNA extends a hand. DESIREE takes it.

EDNA: Shall we have lunch?

DESIREE: I know a really authentic Japanese place—

The door at the rear of the office opens. CJ MORRAN enters.

CJ MORRAN: Well, what have we here?

EDNA: Oh! Miss Morran—what a surprise! You hardly ever get to our end of the building.

CJ MORRAN: Brody, Dugan—what are you doing in Roger's office?

EDNA: We were finishing up a few details on Roger's latest drawing, the Butler Pavilion.

CJ MORRAN: More than likely you two are corrupting his inspired designs. The firm, Morran and Coyne, will be making a few changes.

EDNA: Did you say Morran and Coyne?

CJ MORRAN: I thought I was clear enough.

DESIREE: Roger is to be your partner—?

CJ MORRAN: Yes. What is more, ladies, I have concluded that you two are a distraction to Roger. Therefore, your services are no longer needed.

DESIREE: [**Indignant**] Wha-a-a-t—

EDNA: [**Interrupts quickly**] I beg your pardon, but could you be more explicit, Miss Morran?

CJ MORRAN: With pleasure. BRO-O-DY—YOU ARE FIRED! DUGAN—YOU ARE DISCHARGED! Pick up your final paychecks at personnel and leave the premises IMMEDIATELY!

> **CJ MORRAN does an about face and marches out of the office.**

DESIREE: That hag! Come on, Edna—let's catch up with her in the hallway. I want the pleasure of tearing the paint off her face before I leave.

> **EDNA doesn't move.**

DESIREE: Edna—this is no time to stand there and daydream.

EDNA: Morran and Coyne ... Do you suppose Roger has succumbed to her charms?

DESIREE: We were just fired!

EDNA: You are overreacting. Let's have lunch.

DESIREE: Edna, did you not hear what that woman just said? That play you concocted has been closed before it opened.

EDNA: I heard exactly what CJ said. She said: Brody, you're fired. I am not Brody, I am Brophy. Then she said: Dugan, you are discharged; you are not Dugan, you are Duncan.

DESIREE: But we know what she meant.

EDNA: Who is to know what CJ Morran means? For my part, I simply take her at her word.

DESIREE: Is this how you have survived all these years?

EDNA: Whenever CJ fires you, ask her to be explicit. She invariably fires one of her ex-husbands. Months later she bumps into you in the hallway and says, Brody, are you still with us? And you say, Yes, Miss Morran, busier than ever—and you flutter off.

DESIREE: Edna, you have been an actress all along, haven't you?

EDNA: Darling, it is the only way to survive.

DESIREE: I have underestimated you.

EDNA: Desiree—sister—shall we have lunch?

DESIREE: Shall we try my Japanese place? The tempura is out of this world, best sushi in Hawaii.

> **EDNA and DESIREE exit, chattering and laughing. The state of mind called Honolulu becomes dark.**

INTERLUDE: THE THEATER

> **A dark stage. Spotlight on AMELIA, entering. She addresses the audience.**

AMELIA: Hi, we are back. A lot has happened since we last saw you.

> **Lights up on EDNA and DESIREE, who are engaged in a whispered conversation.**

AMELIA: Edna and Desiree are deeply enmeshed in their comedy, *The Taming of Roger Rogue.* Their object is to get the rogue to surrender—to one of them, of course.

Lights on EDNA and DESIREE go dim, but not entirely down. Lights on ROGER come up. He studies a globe with a magnifying glass.

AMELIA: Instead of surrendering, as any sensible man in his situation would do, Roger's pursuit of freedom is now an obsession. If there is only one place on earth where a man can be absolutely free, he is determined to find it.

Lights on ROGER go down. Lights on LUCRETIA come up. She is annotating a legal document.

AMELIA: Meanwhile, Lucretia in Chicago is working on a scenario of her own: *A Husband Regained.* In sum, all plots and contrivances are now in motion.

Lights on LUCRETIA go down. Edna and Desiree are still seen in a dim light. CJ MORRAN enters, talking.

CJ MORRAN: Plots and contrivances! I call it lunacy! I fired those women! They evaded it on a technicality. And look at what they have done! They have pampered Roger to the point that he is losing his senses. He misses important meetings; and when he does make one, he cannot stop yawning! The planetarium committee is due tomorrow, and his design still is not finished. He assures me that he will be ready, but frankly, I am worried.

AMELIA: You, too, have pampered Roger.

CJ MORRAN: Nonsense! I have simply tried to keep him productive.

AMELIA: You made him a partner in the firm.

CJ MORRAN: That was a mistake. I put the cart before the horse.

AMELIA: [Puzzled] The cart before the—?

CJ MORRAN: Must I explain everything? [Infinitely patient] Marriage is the horse, a partnership is the cart.

AMELIA: I get it. Marriage first, partnership follows.

CJ MORRAN: Until now I have always done it that way. I lost my head.

AMELIA: It is called falling in love.

CJ MORRAN: Amelia, you have been reading too many women's romances. A woman may indulge her heart. I have done that. But when I do, I keep my eyes open. A woman who closes her eyes, even at the height of ecstasy, is—[Searching for a word]—short-sighted.

AMELIA: What you mean is—

CJ MORRAN: Do not correct me! I meant to say blind.

AMELIA: [Sassy] I was going to say happy.

CJ MORRAN: Such impertinence! Amelia, you are fired!!

AMELIA: You can't fire me until we get back to Reality. And when we get there—

CJ MORRAN: —I will forget. [To audience] To know what I know at this moment and realize that it won't do me a bit of good in the future is maddening!

AMELIA: [To EDNA and DESIREE] Are you ready, ladies? [To CJ] If it pains you to watch this, you are free to leave.

CJ MORRAN: Free! What does that word mean? No one has ever defined it. Roger keeps talking about it. He thinks he has achieved it, but the fact is that he's been turned into an absolute fool. I can't bear to watch it. I am leaving.

CJ MORRAN exits. Lights up full on EDNA and DESIREE, their actress selves, in a gossipy frame of mind.

EDNA: Desiree—darling, how did it go?

DESIREE: I have brought Roger to the point of surrender. If you do your job today, he will hoist the white flag tomorrow.

EDNA: Tell me about it.

DESIREE: In the afternoon we surfed. You should take up surfing: it keeps him awake. He dozes at your classical concerts.

EDNA: When he does, he snores, and I nudge him. What happened next?

DESIREE: We had dinner at Philomena's on the pier. While we ate we watched the sun set over the Pacific.

EDNA: I have seen Pacific sunsets. Go on.

DESIREE: After dinner Roger wanted to go home. The poor dear was pooped. I insisted that we go to a jazz club. He didn't want to go, I pouted, then I cried. He had to give in. I kept him up until two A.M. When we got to my apartment he wanted to sleep. I challenged him. "Aren't you up to it?" "Of course I am," he said. He won't admit defeat, so he rose to the occasion—

EDNA: You need not explain further. Where is he now?

DESIREE: At the office.

EDNA: We are going to a concert tonight, then a night club.

DESIREE: Good luck. Bye.

EDNA: Bye.

> **Lights on EDNA and DESIREE go down. Lights up full on ROGER, who has a phone pressed to his ear and a globe of the world mounted on a pedestal before him.**

AMELIA: [**To audience**] True to form, Roger, when cornered, looks for an escape hatch—this time, a rather distant one.

> **Following instructions, ROGER rotates the globe, magnifying glass in hand. He yawns repeatedly as he speaks.**

ROGER: Yes, Mister Iosso, I have a globe in front of me. ... Eighteenth parallel ... one hundred fifty-two longitude ... I am locating it ... I see a lot of little dots ... Eh? ... Ah, yes, of course—the dots are the Island Kingdom: a hundred islands in the sun. Which one is mine? ... Three hundred miles northeast of ... Ah! I see it! It's perfect. What's the price? ... I'll take it! ... You will draw up the papers ... Don't worry about the money. I am on the verge of selling the biggest project of my career—a planetarium. The money is practically in the bank. .... I look forward to seeing you. ... Goodbye.

> **ROGER hangs up the phone. He tries to study the globe, but dozes off. Lights down on ROGER, up on LUCRETIA and PERRY.**

AMELIA: [**To audience**] Meanwhile, in Chicago ...

> **LUCRETIA sets a legal document on PERRY'S desk.**

LUCRETIA: I am sorry, Perry, but this will not do. I refuse to sign it.

PERRY: Lucretia! Roger has agreed to every one of your demands.

LUCRETIA: He has not understood my demands. Nor, apparently, have you.

PERRY: Does Buzz Hapley share your objections?

LUCRETIA: I remind you counselor, that I am a lawyer. I can read a legal document for myself.

PERRY: I did not say you couldn't. But Mr. Hapley is your attorney of record: I thought he might have an opinion. Besides, as your fiancé, I would think he has an interest in seeing your divorce finalized.

LUCRETIA: Mister Hapley's objective is the same as mine: to obtain a satisfactory settlement. This will not do. The wording is too vague. My remarks are in the margins.

PERRY: Lucretia, I undertook this project as a friend—to both you and Roger. I hoped you would be reconciled. But you both assured me that, if reconciliation was not possible, you would be amicable.

LUCRETIA: I am not being hostile, Perry. I merely want to be sure that everything is clear.

PERRY: I don't know what to make of you. You wanted a divorce—insisted on it. Yet you won't let Roger go.

LUCRETIA: [**Indignant**] I am perfectly willing to let him go.

PERRY: Then sign this document. You won't be cheated out of a thing. I think you know that.

LUCRETIA: I am being cheated. Women everywhere are cheated. We are forced to play a game which is not of our making. Those two women in Hawaii are playing Roger's absurd FunBird game, unless— Is he boasting?

PERRY: I can only tell you what he tells me. Both women came to him and said that neither would give him up, so they agreed to share him.

LUCRETIA: They actually did that?

PERRY: That is what Roger told me.

LUCRETIA: They are a disgrace to all women!

PERRY: It's the sun! You get too much of it and you do crazy things.

LUCRETIA: They are doing things which undermine everything that is vital to women. I suppose they are gratifying his every whim.

PERRY: Roger says they ravish him.

LUCRETIA: Ravish?

PERRY: Ravish. His life, he says, is a non-stop round of activity and ecstasy.

LUCRETIA: Really?

PERRY: It won't last. The arrangement Roger has made is unnatural. The last two times I spoke to him, he said he was deliriously happy, but he could not stop yawning.

LUCRETIA: [Aroused] Oh! Oh!! Oh!!! ... Yawning! I see what is happening. Roger thinks that those women are playing his FunBirds game. Do you suppose it is the other way around—that he is playing their game?

PERRY: I don't know. I no longer care. I cared about Roger—the Roger who was my best friend. But that Roger no longer exists. The new Roger—who I have not met but whose voice I hear daily on the phone—is not the same man. He has crossed some kind of divide. When this divorce is finished, I plan to put the new Roger out of my mind. I think it would be best if you did the same thing. Marry Buzz Hapley and get on with your life—your law practice, your kids, your friends.

LUCRETIA: I am not going to marry Buzz.

PERRY: A-a-a-ah.

LUCRETIA: When I first met Buzz, I saw him through tear-stained eyes. My eyes have since cleared up. Perry, something extraordinary is happening to me: I am becoming my real self.

PERRY: [**Alarmed**] Your real self? You sound like Roger! He has told me a hundred times that he has become his real self.

LUCRETIA: In his case it is a delusion.

PERRY: And in yours it isn't? Are you sure of that?

LUCRETIA: I have never told this to anyone, Perry, but a few months before I left Roger, I rescued him from a very embarrassing situation. He was having an affair with two women. One was mature, the other was young.

PERRY: Ah! This FunBird business is not new.

LUCRETIA: No. The only difference is that in Chicago it was covert. Now it is in the open.

PERRY: What was the nature of the embarrassing situation—the one from which you rescued him?

LUCRETIA: I would rather not go into details.

PERRY: Why didn't you leave him right then?

LUCRETIA: I felt that I could set things right. But it wasn't possible. After that episode, Roger could no longer look into my eyes. I had lost him.

PERRY: Then why—if you don't mind my asking—have you been holding up the divorce?

LUCRETIA: I am sorry for what I have put you through, Perry, but Roger's FunBird game no longer upsets me. His love for those women is superficial. I am his real target. He is getting back at me for walking out on him. My intention was to jolt him—bring him to his senses. Instead he did something I didn't expect. He boldly seized the day—started a new life. Audacious, afraid of nothing: that is the Roger I first fell in love with. He was playing the field even then; and he was having his way with women until he met the brown hen—that is how he described me to his bachelor pals. But the brown hen was clever: she reinvented herself, became a beautiful bird and snagged the handsome bachelor. ... The happy years followed. Then slowly she lost him. ... We have come full circle: Roger is once again a free-wheeling bachelor; and the brown hen is once again transforming herself—this time into a Bird of Paradise.

PERRY: [Eyebrows raised] A bird of paradise?

LUCRETIA: The irony of my life—and Roger's—is that, after being married for twenty-two years, he and I are at last ideal partners. How do I get him to realize that? How do I get him to once again be able to look into my eyes?

PERRY: I hate to be a killjoy, Lucretia, but it is too late.

LUCRETIA: It may not be too late. The significant piece of data is that Roger cannot stop yawning. It is possible that he needs to be rescued—again.

PERRY: What are you going to do?

> Deep in thought, LUCRETIA does not respond. The lights on her and PERRY are dimmed. Lights up full on EDNA and DESIREE, who meet hastily.

DESIREE: Edna, that island that Roger wants to buy—I found out where it is. [Rotates the globe] Have a look.

EDNA: Where?

DESIREE: [Points] There.

EDNA: There is nothing there but Pacific Ocean.

DESIREE: Here—use the magnifying glass.

EDNA: All I see are a bunch of little dots ...

DESIREE: Roger is talking about one of those dots. It is one of those grass hut places. No electricity, no nothing. A boat delivers mail and provisions once a month. The last owner was taken by a shark, the one before him by a tidal wave.

EDNA: How did you find that out?

DESIREE: I called Mister Iosso. Edna, what are we to do?

EDNA: Islands are expensive. Can Roger afford it?

DESIREE: He said that he will have the money as soon as he sells the planetarium project.

EDNA: Four other firms are bidding on that project. There is no guarantee—

DESIREE: Every one of Roger's projects has succeeded. He is an irresistible force.

EDNA: Yes, you are right. Something has to be done. Our comedy is coming to an end. The final scene must be as ridiculous as we can make it. ... Don't just stand there! Think of something ridiculous!

DESIREE: Ridiculous?

EDNA: Yes, having to do with Roger.

DESIREE: I know—his shorts. Those things he gets from that men's catalogue.

EDNA: Yes—that's it! [**Paces, thinks**] Yes ... yes, Roger's backside will be the butt of our joke.

DESIREE: If only we could get him to see how ridiculous those things are.

EDNA: I have it!

DESIREE: What is it?

EDNA: A punishment that fits the crime.

> **Lights on EDNA and DESIREE go down. Lights up full on PERRY and LUCRETIA.**

PERRY: Well ... Have you decided?

LUCRETIA: Yes. I have decided to go to Honolulu. I want you to help me.

> **PERRY looks dismayed. Lights down. Spotlight on AMELIA.**

AMELIA: We return to that hermetically sealed world called Reality. It is a day in April, possibly May, but not as late as June.

REALITY: TWO

> **Pointer in hand, ROGER stands beside an easel on which an architectural drawing is mounted. His suit and shirt are wrinkled, his tie is off to one side, his hair is hastily combed, he looks drawn. EDNA is working at Roger's computer. As he addresses his imagined audience, he yawns repeatedly.**

ROGER: In summary, ladies and gentlemen, this will be the first planetarium that is based on relativity theory. Instead of craning his neck to look UP at the dome, the spectator will look DOWN at the heavens. From the standpoint of relativity, it doesn't matter if you are down, looking up, or up, looking down. Seated in a comfortable chair— [sits] which swivels in all directions, there will be a sense of floating in space .. floating ... floating ...

ROGER: [Dozes, awakens] Edna, where are those pills?

EDNA: Which ones?

ROGER: I can't remember the name.

EDNA removes pill bottles from a drawer.

EDNA: The yellow pills are for your allergy—

ROGER: No, not those—

EDNA: —the little blue pills calm you down—

ROGER: That is the last thing I need.

EDNA: The orange pills lower your blood pressure; the green pills steady you; the little pink pills keep you awake.

ROGER: That's it—the pink ones.

EDNA: I will get it for you.

EDNA continues talking as she pours water into a paper cup, and hands cup and tablet to ROGER.

EDNA: I had a wonderful time last night, darling. The Bohemia Quartet was marvelous.

ROGER: It was. But that mad impulse of yours to go to that night club—

EDNA: I will always cherish the memory of it. The two of us on that dark dance floor—clutched in each other's arms, alone on our own blue planet ... Roger, am I boring you?

ROGER: [Wakes up] That pill is having no effect!

EDNA: You have to give it a few minutes.

ROGER: Do you suppose that there is a state of pure exhaustion—one that no tablet can reverse?

EDNA: Roger, you have to rehearse your presentation.

ROGER: [**Rousing himself**] You are right. Back to work. How is the architectural design coming along?

EDNA: I promised I would get it done for you, and I will.

Lights up on CJ MORRAN. Intercom buzzes.

ROGER: Roger Coyne—

CJ MORRAN: Roger, I have been looking at your drawings for the Planetarium. It is a brilliant concept—all that relativity. But I have not found a single rest room, and there is no cafeteria.

ROGER: Those were yesterday's drawings. The rest rooms and cafeteria are being attended to now.

ROGER glances at EDNA, who nods in the affirmative.

CJ MORRAN: You have forgotten a lot of things lately. I am worried about you.

ROGER: There is nothing to worry about. When the rest rooms and cafeteria are installed, I will send the drawings to your printer.

CJ MORRAN: I will be on the lookout for them.

ROGER: By the way, did you get the check for the Butler Pavilion?

CJ MORRAN: It just arrived. You are rich, Roger, disgustingly rich. I have decided to marry you myself—just so I can share some of my own money. Are you divorced yet?

ROGER: I expect to hear from my lawyer today.

CJ MORRAN: Get on with it, Roger. Planetarium first, divorce second. I will call you when I hear from the committee.

CJ MORRAN'S office goes dark. Lights up on AMELIA. Intercom buzzes, ROGER responds.

ROGER: Roger Coyne.

AMELIA: Mr. Coyne, the man from the kingdom called—Mister Iosso.

ROGER: Put him through.

AMELIA: He didn't stay on the phone. He asked me to tell you that he is on his way here from the airport. He has papers for you to sign. He said something about an island—

ROGER: I will want to see him right away, Amelia. Buzz me as soon as he arrives.

AMELIA: Will do, Mr. Coyne.

Lights down on AMELIA. DESIREE enters, carrying a tray with three espresso cups.

DESIREE: Coffee, coffee, coffee. I have made one for you, Edna—a triple espresso for you, Roger, extra strong, one cube of sugar.

EDNA: Thank you, Desiree—that was very thoughtful. Take your time, Roger—don't gulp.

ROGER: There is work to be done.

EDNA: We will get it done.

A conspiratorial glance toward DESIREE

EDNA: Roger, you cannot face a distinguished committee in a suit that looks like you slept in it.

ROGER: I did sleep in it. I fell into bed with my clothes on.

EDNA: Give me the jacket.

> **EDNA helps ROGER slip out of his jacket and hands it to DESIREE. As she does so, she removes a set of keys from the pocket. She lets DESIREE see that she has them.**

EDNA: Desiree, if you would press Roger's jacket, I will install the cafeteria and rest rooms on his design.

DESIREE: Good idea. You practice your presentation, Roger. We will take care of everything else.

ROGER: You are both wonderful. [**An outburst**] Must you be so damned wonderful?

EDNA: It is your idea, Roger. Most men are content with a single supply of wonderful: you have to have two.

ROGER: Ah-hah! So that's your game. You want to force me to choose one of you—that's it, isn't it?

> **EDNA and DESIREE say nothing. DESIREE presses jacket. EDNA works at computer.**

ROGER: I see through your little scheme. All this chumminess between you—it's a plot, isn't it?

EDNA: Is this where the cafeteria is to go, Roger?

ROGER: To the left ... If you two think—There, Edna, stop right there. ... If you think this scheme is going to work, you are very much mistaken. I like things just the way they are. ... Edna, what floor are you on?

EDNA: The second—

ROGER: I want it on the first floor.

EDNA: Don't get upset. It's just a matter of crashing it down one floor.

ROGER: As I was saying, if you two think—

DESIREE: [**A caress**] Darling, you are tired.

ROGER: If you think you can pull the wool—

DESIREE: [**Hugs and kisses**] There, there, you are overwrought. There now, you study your speech. Edna and I will take care of the other things.

Lights up on CJ MORRAN.

ROGER: Vixen! I thought I was free. The fact is that I am trapped. I cannot function without you. I have never in my life taken tablets: now I take five different ones. My clothes are a mess. I—

Intercom buzzes, Roger answers it.

ROGER: Roger—

CJ MORRAN: Roger, the planetarium committee called. They have—all eleven of them—arrived at Honolulu airport. They expect to be here at 6:45 P.M.

ROGER: I will be ready.

CJ MORRAN: I have been checking my printer. Nothing yet.

ROGER: If you keep interrupting—

CJ MORRAN: Roger, the committee has stipulated that we must be ready to make our presentation upon their arrival. If we are not ready, they will turn around and leave.

ROGER: After traveling all the way to Hawaii? Isn't that a bit draconian?

CJ MORRAN: It is one of their ironclad rules. All bidders have the same rules. If you hadn't been dozing so much you might have read them.

ROGER: There is nothing to worry about. We will be ready.

ROGER clicks intercom off. Lights on CJ MORRAN go down.

ROGER: Desiree, hurry with that jacket. Edna, keep going.

EDNA and DESIREE work quietly. ROGER paces, reading his speech sotto voce. Lights on ROGER, EDNA, and DESIREE dim. Lights come up on PERRY and LUCRETIA, who are seated at table in a hotel patio. PERRY, wearing a Hawaiian shirt, has the handset of a phone in his hand.

PERRY: Are you ready?

LUCRETIA: I am afraid. I am all nerves.

PERRY: We have come this far. There is no going back.

PERRY dials. Lights up on AMELIA. Phone rings.

AMELIA: Morran and Selby—

PERRY: Hello, Amelia, this is Perry.

AMELIA: I'll put you through.

PERRY: Thanks.

Lights up on ROGER, who is memorizing his speech.

ROGER: ... into the deepest recesses of the universe ...

Phone rings. ROGER picks it up. Lights down on AMELIA.

ROGER: Roger Coyne.

PERRY: Hello, Roger. It's Perry.

ROGER: I signed those papers. Did you get them?

PERRY: Yes, I did.

ROGER: Good, then it's all set.

PERRY: Well, almost.

ROGER: Almost?

PERRY: Lucretia is willing to sign the papers. Before she does, however, she wants to talk to you.

ROGER: There is nothing to talk about.

PERRY: Roger—as a friend—I advise you to talk to her. She is here with me now.

ROGER: She is—wha-a-t?

PERRY: Will you talk to her, Roger? For old times sake—

ROGER: Are you consorting with our adversary?

PERRY shoves phone into LUCRETIA's hand.

ROGER: Hello? ... Perry ... I asked if you were consorting—

LUCRETIA: Perry is not consorting with anyone. Roger, if you were not such an ingrate, you would appreciate what he has done for you.

ROGER: Lucretia, you have been making my life miserable. Why haven't you signed those papers?

LUCRETIA: Those papers were drafted on the premise that you were entitled to a new life while I continued my old life. The only difference is that I would be Mrs. Hapley instead of Mrs. Coyne. That will not do. Buzz agrees with me. We have decided not to marry.

ROGER: Hurrah! Congratulations! Roger is out of your life, Buzz is out of your life. You are as free as a bird.

LUCRETIA: I am not satisfied with the deal I am getting.

ROGER: I agreed to every one of your demands.

LUCRETIA: I am not talking about demands. There are other issues, personal ones. I would like to discuss them with you—in person.

ROGER: Lucretia, I expect you to sign those papers. If you don't do it, I will get another lawyer and have you all in court. Good bye.

> **ROGER hangs up. Lights on PERRY and LUCRETIA go down.**

ROGER Edna, that cafeteria is standing on its side!

EDNA: I know. I am swinging it around. I will have it in place in a few minutes.

DESIREE: Lucretia is coming—?

ROGER: We can talk about that later. We have work to do.

> **EDNA's hand signals inform DESIREE that Roger is to remove his shirt and pants.**

EDNA: Roger, your clothes are a mess.

DESIREE: The jacket is done. Roger, I need your shirt and pants.

ROGER: You want me to take off my pants—here in the office?

DESIREE: You cannot face a committee of distin-guished citizens in a suit you have slept in. Now give me your pants.

ROGER: A man does not expose his legs in an office.

DESIREE: I have seen your legs before.

EDNA: So have I.

ROGER: But never in the office.

EDNA: Roger, you cannot appear before that committee looking as you do.

ROGER hesitates.

EDNA: Drop your pants immediately. That's an order!

ROGER: You need not be so loud. All right, you can have my pants.

ROGER drops his pants and hands them to DESIREE.

DESIREE: The shirt, too—and the tie.

ROGER: If you insist. [Undoing shirt] Edna, what are you doing to that cafeteria?

EDNA: I am trying to level it. How do you work the leveler in this program?

ROGER: Push Control-Alt-L. Then push the down ar-row until it is level. Then press Shift-Alt-L.

ROGER hands shirt and pants to DESIREE.

DESIREE: Roger, your shorts are wild—absolutely wild!

EDNA: I am amazed that you would wear such flamboy-ant shorts to the office.

ROGER: They are not meant to be seen.

Lights up on AMELIA. Intercom buzzes.

ROGER: [**Pushes button**] Yes—

AMELIA: Mr. Coyne, Mister Iosso is here to see you. He says he has your papers.

ROGER: By all means, Amelia, send him up—

EDNA: [**Points to his shorts**] Roger!

ROGER: Oh! ... Amelia, ask Mister Iosso to have a seat. I will see him shortly.

AMELIA: Very good, Mr. Coyne.

ROGER clicks off. Lights on AMELIA go down.

ROGER: Desiree—what is taking you so long?

DESIREE: I will only be a few minutes—don't be so impatient. Practice your speech.

ROGER: All right—but do hurry. [**Consults notes**] Where was I?

EDNA: There, the design is set.

ROGER: Send it to the printer in CJ's office. ... Desiree, what is taking you so long?

EDNA: I will help Desiree. You practice your speech.

As ROGER begins to address his imaginary audience, EDNA makes a set of gestures indicating that she and DESIREE are to stage a fight over the pants.

ROGER: Ladies and gentlemen—it is a privilege to design a structure in which our spirits soar—

DESIREE: You do the shirt—

ROGER: —in which we leave behind the mundane world—

EDNA: I would rather do the pants.

ROGER: —where mind and spirit are conjoined—

DESIREE: I am no good at shirts, Edna—

ROGER: —and the imagination travels trillions of miles—

EDNA: [**Takes hold of one trouser leg**] Let me do the pants.

ROGER: —in a matter of seconds.

DESIREE: [**Pulls the other trouser leg**] No, Edna—I will do them.

ROGER: And from these vast distances—

EDNA: No, I will—

ROGER: —we gaze back upon our origins—

DESIREE: Me—

ROGER: —we are awestruck—

EDNA: I said ME!!

ROGER: —and we are humbled ...

> **The sound of tearing cloth shatters the atmosphere. EDNA and DESIREE each hold one leg of Roger's pants.**

DESIREE: Look what you have done!

EDNA: That's it—blame me!

DESIREE: Hypocrite!

EDNA: Wench!

ROGER: Edna! Desiree! I have to make a presentation!

Lights up on AMELIA. Intercom buzzes.

ROGER: Yes—

AMELIA: Mr Coyne, Mister Iosso wants to know how soon you will see him.

ROGER: My island—my refuge—it is slipping away from me.

AMELIA: What did you say, Mr. Coyne?

ROGER: Amelia, tell Mister Iosso that I am at the moment indisposed. But don't let him get away. Tell him I am going to consummate the deal.

AMELIA: Very good, Mr. Coyne.

Lights down on AMELIA.

ROGER: Edna—Desiree—I don't care how you do it, but get those pants fixed.

Lights up on CJ. Intercom buzzes. ROGER answers.

ROGER: Yes—

CJ MORRAN: Roger, your drawings just came out on the printer in my office. I am sure they are brilliant. I am sure Picasso was brilliant, though I don't understand a thing he did. If Picasso were to put the rest rooms on the roof of a building and set a cafeteria at a thirty degree angle, people would say he was a genius. In a real building, however—

ROGER: Wha-a-at??!! Give me a few minutes, CJ. I will get it straightened out.

Lights on CJ MORRAN dim, but do not go entirely dark. CJ listens intently to the intercom, which has not been clicked off. ROGER addresses EDNA and DESIREE.

ROGER: The architectural plan is cockeyed; my pants are torn at the crucial moment in my life. It makes no sense. But if you look at it in a certain way, it does make sense.

EDNA: Roger, I have no idea what you are talking about.

DESIREE: You are being absurd!

ROGER: It all started that day when the two of you came to me and said you would share my life. What have you done? You have run me ragged. It is worse than that: you have reduced me to helplessness. And now you have sabotaged my planetarium—and my pants! It is a plot—a conspiracy!

EDNA: Roger, everything we have done is for your benefit.

DESIREE: You are uppermost in our hearts.

ROGER: Everything for my benefit. Who decides what my benefit is? It is a plot—a conspiracy—admit it!

EDNA: We have cooperated with each other—but that is not a plot.

Lights on CJ MORRAN come up full.

CJ MORRAN: [**On intercom**] I have heard enough! Brophy—that is your name, isn't it? Brophy—you are fired! Duncan! You are fired! Both of you are to evacuate the premises immediately. THIS INSTANT!

ROGER: Wait, CJ, you can't do that. I need them ...

EDNA pushes button on intercom. Lights on CJ MORRAN go down.

EDNA: Never mind, Roger. I am tired of this job. I am going to do something else.

ROGER: My pants—

EDNA: To hell with your pants! I don't care about myself. You can't hurt me—I am a survivor. But Desiree is a young woman and I wish you would not string her along the way you do. She won't be young forever. She has to think about making a commitment—a husband, children, family. She cannot fritter her life away.

DESIREE: Thank you, Edna. Roger, I am dropping out. If you had any sense, you would give up this island and marry Edna.

EDNA: No, Desiree, that won't happen. Our comedy— like Roger's—has overreached itself. The result for us is the same as it is for him: dreams become obsessions.

> EDNA and DESIREE embrace.

ROGER: What about my pants!

> EDNA and DESIREE each flail ROGER with a pants leg.

EDNA: Goodbye, Roger

DESIREE: Good luck.

> EDNA and DESIREE exit. ROGER picks up his jacket, then pushes a button on the intercom. Lights up on CJ MORRAN. ROGER searches jacket pockets as he speaks.

ROGER: CJ, the situation is complicated. There is no time to explain. I need a change of clothes. Send Jamie to me. I will have him take a taxi to my apartment and—

CJ MORRAN: Roger, what is going on?

ROGER: Oh, no! They took my keys! Without keys it takes an act of Congress to get into my building.

CJ MORRAN: Did those women leave you naked?

ROGER: I might as well be. Is there a man in the building my size?

CJ MORRAN: It is after five. They have gone home. Roger, the committee will be here momentarily.

ROGER: You will have to make the presentation yourself, CJ. Do the best you can.

> **ROGER pushes intercom button. Lights on CJ MORRAN go down. ROGER pushes second button. Lights on AMELIA up.**

ROGER: Amelia.

AMELIA: Yes, Mr. Coyne.

ROGER: Amelia, would you tell Mister Iosso that I am not well. I will see him tomorrow.

AMELIA: I can't. He left.

ROGER: I told you not to let him go.

AMELIA: A lady arrived. She took Mr. Iosso's card. She said she would call him when you were ready to speak to him.

ROGER: Wha-a-at? Who is this lady?

AMELIA: She did not give her name. She is sitting in the waiting room. She has a large suitcase.

ROGER: A suitcase—?

AMELIA: I believe she is from Chicago.

ROGER: Ah! I see. ... How did this lady get here so fast? I spoke to her less than an hour ago.

AMELIA: I have a suspicion that she was already in Honolulu when she spoke to you.

ROGER: Ah! Perry, too, I suppose. The conspirators are closing in on me from all directions. Amelia, you tell the nice lady that she has wasted her time. I am not seeing her— and that is that.

AMELIA: Oh, Mr. Coyne—must I tell her that?

ROGER: Yes, Amelia—you must. I am not seeing— [An inspiration] Wait. Wa-a-it. Ask the nice lady if she has one of my suits with her.

AMELIA: She told me to tell you—only if you asked— that she packed your grey suit. She also has a white shirt and a tie with red and blue stripes.

ROGER: Damn her! She knew!

AMELIA: Knew what?

ROGER: [Distraught] She knew what would happen ...

AMELIA: I don't understand.

ROGER: There is no time for explanations. Send her up.

AMELIA: Will do.

> ROGER clicks off intercom. Lights on AMELIA go down. ROGER pushes a button. Intercom buzzes. Lights up on CJ MORRAN.

CJ MORRAN: What is it?

ROGER: CJ, I will make that meeting after all. Don't worry about the drawings. I will paint a word picture which will clear up all confusion.

CJ MORRAN: Roger, you are being very erratic, but I am glad you can make it. The committee is in the elevator now.

ROGER: I will be fifteen minutes late. Start talking and keep them entertained until I get there.

Lights on CJ MORRAN go down. ROGER examines the planetarium plan.

ROGER: A place where the spirit soars, where the mind roams freely ...

ROGER looks at himself—at his underwear—and breaks into laughter mingled with tears. The door opens. LUCRETIA enters, carrying a suitcase.

LUCRETIA: Roger, your shorts are a show!

ROGER: What kept you?

LUCRETIA: That is what you said the last time I brought you a change of clothes.

ROGER: I have an important presentation to make.

LUCRETIA: That is the second thing you said the last time. And I said—

ROGER: There isn't time to repeat the conversation verbatim.

LUCRETIA: I said: Be patient. I have them right here.

LUCRETIA, who has opened the suitcase, removes a suit and shirt. ROGER begins to dress.

ROGER: History repeats itself, doesn't it?

LUCRETIA: Not exactly. The last time we played this scene you were stark naked. You needed everything—suit, shirt, tie, underwear, socks, shoes, handkerchief ...

ROGER: Yes, yes. And now I repeat the blunder. There is no fool like an old fool. That is what you are thinking, isn't it?

LUCRETIA: I did not think, say, or imply that you are old.

ROGER: Yes, of course. I should have said a middle-aged fool.

LUCRETIA: Roger, I have never said that you are a fool.

ROGER: You didn't have to say it. You brought my suit— that says it all. You *expected—you knew*—that I would make a fool of myself, just as I did in Chicago.

LUCRETIA: I don't have a crystal ball. I did not know what would happen to you—but I do know you.

ROGER: Oh? Is there something about me that makes women want to expose me naked to the world?

LUCRETIA: Yes, there is.

ROGER: Rea-a-lly? In all our years of marriage you have never once revealed that to me.

LUCRETIA: There was a moment in our lives that you, in your cavalier way, have forgotten. But I have often re-called it.

ROGER: [Trying to recollect] A moment in our lives ... ?

LUCRETIA: It was before we were married. ... The church outing ... the hay ride ...

ROGER: Oh, yes, the romp in the hay loft with the brown hen ... [Recollecting] That was your first time, wasn't it? You were a lot sexier than I thought you would be. [As if struck by lightning] Oh! Oh, yes, I remember: you hid my clothes.

LUCRETIA: Yes.

ROGER: Why?

LUCRETIA: I gave myself to you. It was my first experience.

ROGER: I had the impression that you enjoyed it.

LUCRETIA: I was ecstatic.

ROGER: Then why did you hide my clothes?

LUCRETIA: You were too conceited about your triumph.

ROGER: Conceited! For that you hid my clothes! In fact, you carried it rather far. For a while I thought you were not going to give them back.

LUCRETIA: If I were not in love I would have let the prank go too far. That is what your Chicago FunBirds—what were their names—?

ROGER: I forget.

LUCRETIA: They let the prank go too far.

ROGER: Are you suggesting that they were not in love with me?

LUCRETIA: At the beginning, I am sure they were. But once they got together and compared notes, love turned to cold fury.

ROGER: I don't believe it. They acted on impulse.

LUCRETIA: It was cold calculation. They had it planned in advance.

ROGER: Did they confide in you?

LUCRETIA: No, but I will bet I am right.

ROGER: It is too late to prove anything.

LUCRETIA: We might be able to figure it out—if you are willing to tell me what happened. Thus far, you have been silent on that subject ...

ROGER: [Hesitates, comes to a decision] Do your worst, counselor.

LUCRETIA: All I ask is that you be honest.

ROGER: I will be honest.

LUCRETIA: You were in the conference room. You worked until three A.M. You were tired—very tired. One of those women—my guess is that it was the young one—suggested that a romp on the couch would revive you. You undressed. The older one discreetly left the room. How am I doing?

ROGER: Go on.

LUCRETIA: That is when the phone was removed from the room. The older one had it with her.

ROGER: That is speculative.

LUCRETIA: Roger, the fact is that the phone—the only instrument of communication with the outside world—was removed from the room.

ROGER: Go on.

LUCRETIA: You stretched out on the couch. The young one said she had to go to the ladies room. Am I right?

ROGER: Yes, but that doesn't prove a thing.

LUCRETIA: You fell asleep.

ROGER: Go on.

LUCRETIA: When you awoke, you were alone in the room. Now here is the key question: was the room dark?

ROGER: Why is that a key question?

LUCRETIA: Leaving you in darkness was a sure sign of deadly intent. Well—?

ROGER: The room was pitch black.

LUCRETIA: You groped about. I bet you didn't know where the light switch was.

ROGER: Someone else turns the lights on and off.

LUCRETIA: When you found the door, it was locked. You suddenly experienced fear.

ROGER: I was worried—I admit that.

LUCRETIA: At eight A.M., fifteen of Chicago's most distinguished citizens, among them the mayor, were due to enter that conference room. At 7:40, when I knocked on the door, the voice that said, "Who is it?" was very frightened. Who did you think it was?

ROGER: I thought it was Fran or Diana—those were their names. I thought they were calling off the joke—giving me back my clothes.

LUCRETIA: But it wasn't them, Roger. It was your wife.

ROGER: Yes, yes. It was my wife. ... I still say they re-lented. You have not been honest with me. I would bet that one of them called you and said that I would need clothes.

LUCRETIA: Neither of them called.

ROGER: I refuse to believe that you just divined that I was locked naked in a conference room.

LUCRETIA: I didn't divine anything. When you had not come home all night, I figured that something was wrong. I called your office. The phone rang and rang. No answer. It was before office hours, but if you were there, you would have answered. It wasn't difficult to figure out that you were having an affair. Something was wrong. I recalled the hay ride. I remembered the temptation I experienced.

ROGER: Do you have a tie?

LUCRETIA hands ROGER a necktie.

ROGER: There is something I need to know. Perhaps you would help me. What is it about me that makes women want to humiliate me in this particular way?

LUCRETIA: There is something about you, Roger—something that evokes a peculiar feminine demon.

ROGER: A demon—?

LUCRETIA: A demon that compels a woman to teach a man a lesson. It is a woman thing. She attacks his weakness—his vanity.

ROGER: And my vanity is—?

LUCRETIA: You dress meticulously. It is the facade you present to the world. It is of crucial importance to you. What does a woman do to a debonair man—if she is in a vindictive mood?

ROGER: She removes the facade.

LUCRETIA: Exactly.

ROGER: Thank you, Lucretia. I have learned something from you. From now on I will dress casually.

LUCRETIA: That won't work, Roger. There are other demons—even more terrible ones.

ROGER: [Checks watch] I have a meeting to attend.

LUCRETIA: It can wait a few more minutes.

ROGER: What do you want?

Instead of answering the question, LUCRETIA examines the planetarium design.

LUCRETIA: What an odd building. What are those structures on the roof?

ROGER: Cosmic outhouses. I am on my way to explain the whole thing to a distinguished committee. It will be either a total disaster or the greatest success of my career. If it is a failure, I shall disappear somewhere. If it is a success, CJ and I will join the committee for dinner. Amelia can help you get a taxi to your hotel. There is no time for fond farewells. Good luck. [At the door] By the way, thanks for delivering the laundry.

LUCRETIA: Roger, you have not once looked into my eyes. Would you do it now, please.

ROGER complies, though it requires all the courage he can muster.

ROGER: What do you want?

LUCRETIA: I am not going back to Chicago.

ROGER: You didn't answer my question. What do you want?

LUCRETIA: You.

ROGER: It won't work. We have been through too much.

LUCRETIA: We have done good things. We have children. They love us, we love them.

ROGER: That is all lost.

LUCRETIA: Nothing that was good is lost.

ROGER: It was the old Roger who was part of that good. You are talking to the new Roger.

LUCRETIA: I like the new Roger. He is very much like the original Roger, the man I fell in love with. ... Let's try it again.

ROGER: It is too late. I am a new man. I cannot go back.

LUCRETIA: I am a new woman. I am prepared to go forward. The only thing I want from the past is something exquisitely beautiful. I remember when you could look straight into my eyes and say, "I love you." And my answer was always the same: "Roger dearest, I love you more than life itself." When I spoke those words, I meant them.

> **LUCRETIA takes ROGER's hand. He is very nearly captivated, but breaks off to check his watch.**

ROGER: I am late! Those people are waiting for me. I have to run.

> **ROGER dashes off.**

LUCRETIA: Yes, Roger, run. Run, run ... run ... run ...

> **Disconsolate, LUCRETIA pushes a button on the intercom. Buzzing sound. Lights up on AMELIA.**

AMELIA: Yes, Lucretia.

LUCRETIA: Amelia, those women—Edna and Desiree—do you know where they are? I would like to meet them.

AMELIA: I will see if they are still in the building. Heidi in personnel told me that Miss Morran fired them.

LUCRETIA: Oh—

AMELIA: Do you still want to see them?

LUCRETIA: Yes ... Yes, I think I had better see them.

AMELIA: If I can locate them, I will ask them to stop by.

LUCRETIA: Thanks, Amelia.

AMELIA: While you are waiting, would you like to hear your husband's presentation to the planetarium committee? I am taping it for Miss Morran. You can hear it on the intercom.

LUCRETIA: All right, Amelia. Thank you.

Light on AMELIA goes down. Lights up on ROGER, who is in a CJ Morran's space.

ROGER: Seated in a chair that rotates slowly, the spectator will feel as though he is an object in space. As he travels deeper and deeper into the void, he finds that he is shaking off his fetters. He has a sense that he and the universe are one ...

EDNA and DESIREE enter.

LUCRETIA: Thank you for coming ladies—

ROGER: He is bound only by nature's laws. His human shackles—the laws, the conventions—have been thrown off. ...

LUCRETIA: Excuse me.

LUCRETIA turns down volume on intercom. Lights on ROGER dim.

LUCRETIA: You, I take it are Desiree. And you are Edna. I am Lucretia.

DESIREE picks up a leg from Roger's torn trousers.

DESIREE: What is Roger wearing?

LUCRETIA: His best suit. I brought it for him.

EDNA: [**Incredulous**] You packed his suit?

LUCRETIA: This is not the first time Roger has been stripped by women. It is a punishment he seems to invite.

EDNA and DESIREE look at each other, astonished.

EDNA: He has played this comedy in the past—?

LUCRETIA: Twice that I know of.

DESIREE: Are you saying that my aristocrat is a fool?

LUCRETIA: That is a question we must never ask. If he is a fool, what are we who pursue him?

EDNA: You want him back ...

LUCRETIA: I already own him. He is my husband.

EDNA: That is a technicality. You are a character in a comedy called *FunBirds*, the woman from the past. We brought Roger's comedy to an ignominious close. You revived it. You gave him an opportunity to sell his planetarium.

DESIREE: Shall we see how he is doing?

DESIREE turns up the volume on the intercom. Lights on ROGER come up.

ROGER: To answer your question, sir, the usual practice is to put restrooms in out-of-the-way places. According to Relativity, up and down have no special significance. When we look DOWN at the heavens, our rest rooms might as well be UP—on the roof. In fact, ladies and gentlemen, yours will be the world's first planetarium with cosmic lounges. ... As for the cafeteria, setting it at angle is one of the greatest inspirations of my career. By an ingenious use of ramps, the angular space will accommodate twenty percent more tables than a horizontal space.

Applause is heard. DESIREE clicks intercom off. Lights on ROGER go down.

DESIREE: Bravo, rogue.

EDNA: It sounds to me like Roger has just made that sale. He will have the money to buy his island.

LUCRETIA: Island? Oh, yes, the one Mister Iosso spoke of. I met him in the reception room.

DESIREE: It is a speck in the South Pacific. Roger plans to live there.

LUCRETIA: He would be bored to tears in a month.

DESIREE: Perhaps, but at the moment that is his dream.

LUCRETIA: You wouldn't go with him, would you?

DESIREE: If the island had electricity—and I was his only FunBird—I would go.

LUCRETIA: You are young, Desiree. Your life is ahead of you. It is very romantic to talk about going to a tropical island with a man who is twenty years older than you are. Would you actually do it?

DESIREE: I would have two children—maybe three. If I were to survive Roger, I would be better able to face those bleak years than if I settled down with someone my age who—mentally, emotionally—is ten years younger than I am.

LUCRETIA: I see. ... And you, Edna?

EDNA: Iampasthavingachild, butiftheislandwashabitable—
and there was enough money in the bank to guarantee my
future in the event Roger changed his mind—I would jump
at it.

DESIREE: What about you, Lucretia?

LUCRETIA: A tropical island would be a bit much, but
I expect that I would talk him out of it. **[Pause]** ... I hated
the women who made a fool of my husband in Chicago. I
should hate you, Edna, and you, Desiree—but I don't. In
fact, I rather admire you.

DESIREE: Does that mean you are giving up the pursuit
of Roger?

LUCRETIA: No. I am as competitive as any woman. I
merely—

ROGER bursts into the office. He is ebullient.

ROGER: Congratulate me, ladies. I made the sale!

LUCRETIA: Congratulations. Roger, we need to talk.

ROGER: Not now. CJ and I are taking the planetarium
committee to dinner.

EDNA: CJ can wait.

DESIREE: The committee can wait.

ROGER: Edna, Desiree, after the way you treated me, I
have nothing to say to you.

DESIREE: Come, Roger, we treated you exactly as you
treated us. If we were characters in your comedy, we were
entitled to make you a character in our comedy.

EDNA: Lucretia has introduced a new comedy. It is
called, *What Will Roger Do?* We are now playing it. There

are four characters: you and three women who have made extraordinary emotional investments in you.

ROGER: I see ... [A deep breath, sits] To the world, I am the best of men. You three—you only—have found me out. I am amazed that any of you would want me.

EDNA: You are being evasive, Roger. We want no more of that. We want you to talk to us. We don't want to hear Roger, the actor: we want to hear the voice of the real Roger.

ROGER: What shall I talk about?

DESIREE: Us.

ROGER: Very well, I will talk about you. ... I love Desiree—her youth, her vitality, her love of life. ... But I would miss Edna terribly—her music, her sense of humor, her ability to put things in perspective. ... Lucretia is the woman incarnate. The Brown Hen who sees my very soul. Can I live without her? ... It is too complicated. I long for an elemental life.

DESIREE: The island you were going to buy?

ROGER: No. It won't do. My island will have a few villages, palm trees, a sublime beach.

DESIREE: With one companion ...

ROGER: [Resigned] Yes, one companion.

There is a subtle but noticeable change in the stage lighting.

EDNA: Who?

ROGER: I— ... I can't ... I honestly cannot decide.

World-weary, ROGER leans back and closes his eyes.

DESIREE: It is obvious that he can't decide. ... Roger, how about if we settle it?

ROGER: Yes. Yes, I suppose that would be best.

> Lights up on AMELIA and PERRY, who watch the ensuing scene with some amusement. The atmosphere begins to change: only ROGER seems to notice it. He peers out in the direction of the audience as though trying to see forms emerging from a fog. He smiles. Meanwhile, LUCRETIA, DESIREE and EDNA are preoccupied with the business of how to settle the matter.

LUCRETIA: [To Desiree] You expect us to settle the matter. Do you have any notion as to how it might be done?

> Desiree fishes three dice out of her pocket.

DESIREE: I have three dice. Ladies, pick your color.

LUCRETIA: Do you propose to settle our futures with a throw of dice?

EDNA: If you think about it Lucretia, throwing dice is more rational than the methods we now use to select mates. Will you accept the result, Roger?

> ROGER, who has been preoccupied with the atmospheric change, smiles shrewdly and says—

ROGER: Yes, I will accept it.

DESIREE: I would suggest that we each roll our own die.

LUCRETIA: This is madness!

EDNA: Do you have a better way?

> LUCRETIA stares incredulously at EDNA and DESIREE, looks at ROGER, and mutters—

LUCRETIA: Insane ... Insane ... [**Lucretia laughs, laughs again, then says—**] I'll take the jade one.

EDNA: I'll take the chartreuse.

DESIREE: That leaves me with the red one. How shall we settle it? Highest number wins?

EDNA: No. Number three wins.

DESIREE: That's your lucky number, isn't it?

EDNA: Yes. How is it with you Lucretia?

LUCRETIA: Three is as good a number as any.

DESIREE: Ready? One, two, throw ...

> **The dice are rolled.**

EDNA, DESIREE, LUCRETIA: I win!!!

DESIREE: Can you believe it? We all rolled a three. Shall we try again? This time, highest number wins.

> **LUCRETIA and EDNA nod their acquiescence. Again the dice are rolled.**

EDNA, DESIREE, LUCRETIA: I win!!!

DESIREE: We all rolled a six. What is going on? Have the laws of probability been suspended?

AMELIA: Roll the dice as often as you like. Every time you do, each character's wish shall be fulfilled. Your time is up. You are back in the theater.

> **The change in lighting is now complete. It is the same light we had seen at the outset: light without substance. Upon AMELIA's signal, the characters face the audience as they did in the Prelude.**

POSTLUDE: THE THEATER

AMELIA: [**Addresses audience.**] Ladies and gentlemen, before you decide how things will turn out, our characters have a few things to say. [**Shuffles four cards**] Roger will be the first to speak, then Edna; Lucretia is third, Desiree last.

EDNA: Why do you bother using those cards? The result always comes out the same.

AMELIA: I consult the cards to see what the gods of chance have to say. If I don't like the result, I remember that I am the boss. ... Roger, you are first..

ROGER steps forward, addresses audience

ROGER: The moment we dread has arrived: we cease to be. But we do not perish. We live on in your minds and imaginations. Most stage characters—those whose fate is sealed at the end of the play—are quickly forgotten. But not us. Today you will decide our futures; or perhaps you will defer the decision. But you will always be aware that my life—like your own—is a destiny in progress. From time to time you will think of me and say, "I wonder what Roger is doing?"—and you will update my story. I ask only one thing: whatever you have me doing, have me passionately involved in it. ... Enough said. Adieu.

EDNA: That was a pretty speech, but I hope you will not let Roger off the hook. He has obligations to fulfill. For my own part, I do not expect a romantic ending. The world has changed: romance is out of fashion. But the world has not been turned upside down. We still think of men as being handsome, women as beautiful. In spite of my frustrations with him, Roger has made me aware that I am a beautiful woman. I see it in his eyes. They are the mirrors of my soul. Beautiful. That is why I want him. True, the risks are great, but you, my friends, can set things straight.. ... Thanks.

LUCRETIA: When you conclude this comedy, I would suggest that you focus your attention not on us—the women in the story—but on Roger. It is time to put *him* under the microscope. What do you suppose Roger will do? In theory he has a hundred options; in fact, he has only one. Ask yourselves: can Roger be happy without a strong woman in his life—a woman who is not a mere FunBird? She will, of course, put her heart and soul into the relationship. ... Do I want him? Yes—on one condition: that he can look into my eyes and say, "I love you."... I am not appealing to your sentiments: I am merely setting forth my terms. I don't expect sentiment. Playwrights are notoriously unsentimental. They prefer to settle things with a plot twist. Do you suppose that Roger will once again need to be rescued? There is your twist—and your ending. Thank you.

DESIREE: Ladies and gentlemen, you are not only playwrights, you are an audience. The best ending to a comedy is one that satisfies the expectations of its audience. Ask yourselves: what dream has this comedy been striving toward? Don't try to think it out logically. Instead, set an image in your mind: a tropical island, palm trees, coconut groves, villages in which people lead utterly simple lives. Imagine the vast Pacific Ocean, in which this island is a refuge. And on that island is a man who has renewed his life, who has become a bronze god under a blazing sun. At his side, there is a woman—a young woman, a bronze goddess. Envision that man and woman strolling hand in hand, barefoot on a beach, their feet washed by crystalline waters; imagine them gazing upon the sun as it drops beneath the horizon and colors sky and ocean in progressively deepening shades of red. Think of them fulfilling nature's dictum: living simple lives, lovers in each other's warm embrace—in love with each other, in love with life. Resolve our story into the dream it has sought to become, and the recollection of it will add joy to your remaining days. Aloha.

AMELIA: [**To audience**] Well, we have had our say. And so we bid you—

CJ MORRAN enters, talking.

CJ MORRAN: Roger, the planetarium committee is not only impatient, they are starved! I have gotten nowhere on the intercom, so I have come myself to fetch you. **[Surveys the scene]** Brody, Dugan, are you still here? **[Stares at LUCRETIA]** Who are you?

LUCRETIA: I am Mrs. Coyne.

CJ MORRAN: Mrs—! Roger! Aren't you divorced yet?

ROGER: It takes time, CJ. It takes time.

CJ MORRAN: I can't believe that a man of your energy cannot settle a simple matter like a divorce. I— **[Catches sight of audience]** WHO ARE THESE PEOPLE?

ROGER: They are the playwrights. They will decide how our story is to turn out.

CJ MORRAN: Oh! Oohh! Oh, yes, I quite forgot. **[To audience, an ingratiating smile]** You are the ones we met at the beginning. It is nice to see you again. Now, being new to the playwriting business, I suppose you will want a little advice. The first thing to do is get Roger to go with me to have dinner with the planetarium committee before we lose that contract. WE NEED THE MONEY! After that, Roger's future needs to be attended to. For all his failings, Roger is a genius—the Picasso of architecture. Who but a genius could persuade a distinguished committee that the proper place for a toilet is on the roof? But Roger will not be happy unless he is married—to the right woman, of course. I happen to be the right woman—and I NEED A HUSBAND! Under this hard executive exterior is a heart that yearns to be consoled. **[Squints at audience]** I suppose a few of you ladies are muttering under your breaths that I have had more than my share of husbands. The difference between you and me is that you have searched, I have searched in vain. I, too, am entitled to a happy ending. Now, here is your ending. Roger gets his divorce, marries me, cements his position as partner in the firm—and consoles a loving wife. Thank you. [A no-nonsense smile] Oh, yes, there is one thing you must not forget: Roger will be a partner in the firm, but I am the *senior* partner. Thank you so much.

AMELIA: [To audience] Well, ladies and gentlemen, I suppose that does it.

IMPROVISATION

There is a mood of feminine discontent—an imminent explosion.

EDNA: Just a minute! I am not satisfied.

WOMEN'S VOICES: Neither am I ... Nor me ... It is all wrong ...

EDNA: Roger will be a featured player in every ending. I get to play in one of four.

WOMEN'S VOICES: True, true ... it is not fair ... a bad deal ...

EDNA: Ladies, I am prepared to play a comedy called *All-or-Nothing*.

DESIREE: One of us gets the prize, the others look elsewhere. I will go along with that.

LUCRETIA: Roger, there still is time.

ROGER: Time? For what?

LUCRETIA: For you to decide this matter for yourself.

DESIREE, EDNA, LUCRETIA and CJ MORRAN converge on ROGER.

ROGER: [Wary] Ladies ...

DESIREE: We are tired of playing your comedy.

EDNA: Only you can bring it to a permanent close.

ROGER: CJ, we have business to attend to.

CJ MORRAN: It can wait long enough for you to say the magic words, Roger.

LUCRETIA: If you don't do it, the audience will have another look at you—in your birthday suit.

DESIREE: We will strip you.

EDNA: Our playwrights will see you exactly as you are.

Desperate, ROGER looks about for an avenue of escape.

CJ MORRAN: There is no escape, Roger.

PERRY and AMELIA watch the scene, bemused, as four ladies converge on ROGER.

ROGER: Ladies ... ladies ... ladies ... ladies ... LADIES, BE REASONABLE!!!

In desperation, ROGER removes a picture from the wall, revealing a hidden wall panel. He grasps a large electric switch and pulls it.

BLACKOUT

THE WISDOM PART

Spotlights come up at stage front. PERRY and AMELIA appear.

PERRY: We live, we don't learn.

AMELIA: But we never stop trying.

PERRY: A philosopher once said that each of us has a history that extends back to the dawn of time.

AMELIA: Unfortunately, we cannot recall it.

PERRY: Which explains the fact that we don't learn from past mistakes.

AMELIA: But we must never give up! We must try again and again until we get it right.

PERRY: Do you suppose that Roger and his ladies will ever get it right?

AMELIA: We must believe that one day it will happen.

PERRY: [**To audience**] Perhaps if you were to see tomorrow's show ...

AMELIA: Do come, but there are no guarantees and NO REFUNDS.

PERRY: [**To AMELIA, then to audience**] Good night, good night.

> **AMELIA** addresses **Perry,** the audience, then **DIONYSIUS.**

AMELIA: Good night, good night, aloha.

BLACKOUT

FINI

THE PEACE CONFERENCE AT BILLOP HOUSE, SEPTEMBER 11, 1776

The only attempt to negotiate a settlement of the American Revolutionary War

DRAMATIS PERSONAE

Narrator

Admiral Lord Richard Howe Commander, British Naval
Forces in America

Benjamin Franklin of Pennsylvania

John Adams of Massachusetts

Edward Rutledge of South Carolina

British and Hessian Troops, Oarsmen

THE PLACE

The Billop House on Staten Island, NY

THE TIME

Midday, Friday, September 11, 1776

Eager to have a look at famous American rebels, a crowd gathered on the beach watches a small boat in mid-channel, half way between Perth Amboy, New Jersey, and Staten Island, New York. The boat lands. Enthusiastic Colonial volunteers pull the boat up on to the shore. JOHN ADAMS, EDWARD RUTLEDGE and BENJAMIN FRANKLIN step on to the beach. They are followed by a British Officer in a red coat. As they advance toward ADMIRAL HOWE, who awaits them on the great lawn, British and Hessian troops stake positions aligning the path they will take to the Conference House. Drum roll, music.

NARRATOR: The year is 1776, the pivotal year in America's struggle for independence. Americans in all thirteen colonies are in rebellion against British rule. The Continental Army, under the command of George Washington, is engaging British forces in Massachusetts, New York, and New Jersey. Colonists everywhere are acting in defiance of British authority. British reprisals have only stiffened colonial opposition.

On July 4th, Americans took the decisive step: representatives from all the American colonies signed the Declaration of Independence. The British response was to send a large military expedition to quell the rebellion. Admiral Richard Howe was in charge of British naval forces; his brother William had command of the army.

A gesture indicating Howe, who is standing in a position halfway between the conference house and the shore, waiting to greet the colonists as they approach.

Admiral Howe believed that a negotiated peace was possible; he was granted permission by King George III to attempt a settlement. He wrote a letter to a number of distinguished Americans, offering to seek a peace agreement. He hoped especially for a response from Benjamin Franklin, with whom he was friendly during Franklin's days as Colonial Representative in London.

Franklin introduced Howe's letter at a session of the Continental Congress which then met in Philadelphia. The Congress authorized Franklin, John Adams of Massachusetts and Edward Rutledge of South Carolina, to meet Admiral Howe to determine if he had anything of substance to offer.

The meeting took place in a substantial stone building, known as the Billop House after its original owner, Captain Christopher Billop. Let us imagine that this is the very day they met: Friday, September 11th, 1776. It is a meeting of enemies under a flag of truce. The flag is essential. If captured, the three Americans would be tried and hanged as traitors. On this occasion, however, Admiral Howe guaranteed their safety.

The American delegation needed two days to travel from Philadelphia to Perth Amboy, New Jersey. They traveled by coach over rough roads, stopping now and then to take a meal and stretch aching limbs. They stopped overnight in New Brunswick. Rooms being scarce, Franklin and Adams had to share a small room with a single bed.

Perth Amboy—just across the river—is held by Colonial rebels. Staten Island is a British fortress: 32,000 British Redcoats and Hessian mercenaries are stationed here. The sounds of cannon shots fired from one side of the river to the other is a daily routine.

As proof of his good intentions, Admiral Howe sent one of his officers as a hostage to be held by American forces until the delegation returned to Perth Amboy. The Americans, believing that Howe would be true to his word, had the hostage cross the narrows with them.

Let's join Admiral Howe as he greets the American delegation.

Fanfare, musket salute as the colonial delegation approaches. Howe recognizes the officer he had sent to act as a hostage.

HOWE: Gentlemen, you bring my hostage with you. You pay me a high compliment, and you may depend upon it, I will consider it the most sacred of things.

FRANKLIN: We have every confidence in your honor, your lordship.

HOWE: For that I thank you. ... I trust that your journey was reasonably comfortable.

ADAMS: It was as comfortable as it might be, your lordship, considering that last night I shared a bed with Dr. Franklin, a man whose bulk is superior to my own. I did manage to get a night's sleep, though I am the victim of one of his faulty theories.

HOWE: [In decidedly good humor] I know Franklin well: we played chess together in London. He is a man of active mind and numerous theories. But which of his theories are you alluding to?

ADAMS: His theory of catching and avoiding colds. He insisted upon opening the window in our room on a rather chilly night. Fresh air, he said, keeps off colds. His theory is wrong. I started the night with a slight cold, and by morning it was a bad cold.

FRANKLIN: Adams, I say that my theory is correct. I did not catch your cold.

HOWE: Ah-hah! Always a retort! I see that my old friend is as quick-witted as ever. But I have not had the pleasure of meeting the third member of your party.

RUTLEDGE: I am Edward Rutledge from South Carolina.

HOWE: [Dour] South Carolina has not been kind to His Majesty's royal governors.

RUTLEDGE: Nor have the governors been kind to South Carolina.

HOWE: With a little good will those grievances can soon be forgotten. But come, gentlemen, before we talk we have prepared a repast for you.

HOWE's gesture indicates that they are to walk alongside him toward the Conference House. As the four men walk together, the Narrator speaks.

HOWE: At this point, Admiral Howe invited his guests to enter the Conference House where a table laden with food awaited them. The menu included good claret, ham, tongue and mutton. After the luncheon, they sat about a large table and began their discussion.

HOWE, FRANKLIN, ADAMS and RUTLEDGE take places at a table.

HOWE: I hope you have enjoyed our modest menu, gentlemen. This being a military camp, we are unfortunately not able to match our London tables.

FRANKLIN: We are colonials, quite accustomed to plain food. Your lordship has fed us beyond our expectations. It has been a veritable feast.

HOWE: Not the last feast, I hope.

Pause as HOWE composes himself. He is now the King's representative, a status which confers upon him the authority of Empire.

HOWE: Now, may I ascertain in what official capacities are you here?

FRANKLIN: We are representatives appointed by the Congress to hear your proposals.

HOWE: [Peremptory] You must not mention Congress. I cannot deal with a congress. His Majesty does not recognize your congress. The very mention of it puts him into a fit. [Conciliatory, in a brusque sort of way] But when everything is settled and the colonies are once again restored to their proper places in the British Empire, there will be no need for a congress.

FRANKLIN: Your lordship may consider us in any view you think proper. We are at liberty to consider ourselves in our real character. The conversation may be held as among friends.

ADAMS: I am willing to consider myself in any character which would be agreeable to your lordship—except that of a British Subject.

HOWE: [Mordant] Mr. Adams is a decided character.

RUTLEDGE: I think, with Dr. Franklin, that the conversation may be as among friends.

HOWE: A conversation among friends it shall be.

> Pause as HOWE searches for words.

HOWE: In spite of our disagreements, we British are kindly disposed toward Americans. When an American falls, England feels it. I feel the same even more strongly. If America fell, I should feel and lament it like the loss of a brother.

FRANKLIN: [A slight bow, an easy air, a sly smile.] We will do our utmost to spare your lordship that mortification.

> HOWE is a bit nonplused at that remark. It is Franklin that he is most counting on, the Franklin he knew in London.

HOWE: Come, come, Dr. Franklin, the issues that divide us are trivial. Surely we can reach an accommodation—reunite our countries and peoples under terms satisfactory to both.

ADAMS: Reunite? Surely your lordship is aware that we have declared independence.

HOWE: **[Irritable]** A rash decision—made in the heat of passion! When calm is restored, I am sure you will reconsider it. Besides—to put it plainly—I cannot discuss independence. His Majesty wants that word banished from dictionaries in all our colonies; it may be retained if it is defined as a plague.

FRANKLIN: The Declaration of Independence was proclaimed a little over two months ago, on July fourth. It followed America's last petition to the King. The King's response to that petition was to send out forces and burn our towns.

ADAMS: The Declaration of Independence is not simply an act of rebellion. It sets forth an ideal that is now universally desired in our colonies. It is not in our power, my lord, to treat our colonies as anything other than independent states. For my own part, I vow never to depart from the idea of independence.

HOWE: Mr. Adams! I can understand why you are not liked in London.

ADAMS: To be disliked in London is to me a badge of honor.

RUTLEDGE: May I interrupt this badinage?

HOWE: Please do, Mr. Rutledge.

RUTLEDGE: I am one of the longest-serving members of Congress, my lord, having been a member from the beginning. I am glad this conversation is taking place: it will be the occasion of opening to Great Britain the advantages she would derive from an alliance with a free America. Trade with America would enrich English commerce, provide employment for its people and revenues for its government. We can protect the West India islands more effectively than England can, to say nothing of the Newfoundland fishery.

HOWE: Highly desirable! But all that can be achieved under the benevolent protection of the British Empire. Besides, there is more to it than commerce: the British Empire must protect her subjects and yes, her interests, in many parts of the world. America can confer upon Great Britain solid advantages; it is her commerce, her strength, her men, that we chiefly want.

FRANKLIN: We are a considerable manufactory of men, My lord, but they are increasingly unwilling to fight Britain's wars.

ADAMS: And they are angered by the fact that American sailors are seized on the high seas and shanghaied into the British navy.

HOWE: Your sailors are British subjects. They can be called to serve in our navy.

ADAMS: Our sailors, their friends and families, take it to be kidnaping!

HOWE: [Conciliatory] That will change if we can reach an agreement. When that is done, colonials will willingly fight side-by-side with British soldiers and sailors. There have been what you call abuses: impressment of sailors, taxation and other issues. These can be remedied. Detached from the British Empire, your colonies will soon be at war with one another. As members of the Empire, a wise and benevolent government will maintain harmony.

> The following is spoken not in anger, but rather as an attempt to persuade the representative of an old order that a sea-change in human affairs is at hand.

RUTLEDGE: Fine sentiments, my lord, and I know you utter them sincerely. But, on this continent—except for isolated Tory centers—the old loyalties no longer hold. A large and ever-increasing number of Americans do not think of themselves as British subjects. They will no longer consent to come again under English government. I can answer for South Carolina. The royal government was very oppressive. At last we took the government into our own hands and the people are now settled and happy under that government. Under no circumstances will they return to the King's government.

HOWE: [Huffy] A very uncompromising statement, sir. But consider the alternative, which is to restore his Majesty's government by force of arms. A war will last for years and will devastate your societies. It is that which I hope to avoid. But this cannot be achieved unless *all parties* are prepared to compromise.

FRANKLIN: May we hear what compromises your lordship is authorized to offer us?

HOWE: His Majesty is most generous. He is prepared to issue a blanket pardon to all rebels.

ADAMS: All? Friends of mine who are close to your government have informed me that there is a secret protocol to this effect: that John Adams' pardon shall take the form of a rope around his neck.

HOWE: You have managed to annoy quite a few people in London, Mr. Adams. I don't deny it. But I know of no secret protocol.

ADAMS: I take your Lordship at his word. I will nonetheless be cautious.

HOWE: To continue with His Majesty's agenda: a fair settlement of tax grievances and the restoration of representative government that serves its people, is loyal to His Majesty, and which preserves a great Empire. All in all, a sensible solution.

FRANKLIN: If I were to tell the citizens of any of our colonies that the King proposed to pardon them, I would be a laughing stock—and I might well find myself in the stocks. Our citizens are of the opinion that His Majesty ought to apologize to them. His armies have burnt defenseless towns in the midst of winter, and he is now bringing foreign mercenaries to deluge our settlements with blood.

HOWE: [His blood up, but containing himself.] It is rebellion that has brought about such harsh measures! ... Gentlemen, we are civilized men. We are here to find a way to end the ruinous extremities which follow upon rebellion.

FRANKLIN: As you know, your lordship, I have in the past thought that reconciliation was possible. When I was in England, we spoke of it often. That was years ago. Things have changed. We have progressed too far along the path of independence. For us, there is no turning back. Might I suggest a different compromise. Perhaps your lordship would send home for authority to negotiate with us as an independent nation.

HOWE: That is a vain hope.

Pause. It is over. They all know it.

HOWE: I appreciate your candor, gentlemen, but it is clear to me now that no accommodation is possible. The war will go on. You will suffer greatly, and in the end you cannot prevail. Just recently General Washington's army was soundly thrashed in Long Island. We could see how ragged, half-starved, poorly equipped, and undisciplined his men were. Our agents report that his men leave when their recruitments expire; quite a few others desert. That does not sound like a population desirous of independence. A prolonged war will cause a great deal of starvation and misery. And, if you lose the war, the terms will be much harsher.

ADAMS: In Long Island, we lost a battle, your lordship, but not a war. Our territory is vast, our people seized with the idea of liberty. A million British troops and Hessians cannot conquer them.

FRANKLIN: Defeat us in one place, and rebellions will pop up in a dozen other places.

RUTLEDGE: A prolonged war will cost England dearly. You will deplete your treasury and impoverish your own subjects. Trade with us as equal partners, and you will prosper. We will all prosper.

Pause. HOWE contemplates the men sitting opposite him who are obviously resolute.

HOWE: There is, I suppose, no more to be said. I wish you a safe journey back to your homes and hope that we will meet again in happier circumstances.

FRANKLIN: Adieu, my Lord. We thank you for your equanimity and your hospitality.

A disappointed Howe signals the militia. Several men led by an officer form an escort column. The group marches toward the beach and the skiff that will take them back to Perth Amboy.

NARRATOR: To some historians, the conference on Staten Island was a minor incident. Nothing significant happened: no deal was reached. But something significant did happen: no deal was reached. Three Americans resisted the temptation to compromise the ideal of liberty. As they boarded the barge that would take them back to Perth Amboy, they knew that the coming years would test America's mettle. But there was something else—something more profound: their conversation with Admiral Howe made him aware that a sea-change was occurring in the affairs of men. The world would never be the same.

HOWE: Oh Empire! We have won many battles for you; and as we have grown older, we have had reason to wonder why we fought—even to regret our victories. Now it is their turn. They will win. And they, too, will grow old.

Music. A slow march, then bagpipes and lively music.

FINI

www.ingramcontent.com/pod-product-compliance
Lightning Source LLC
Chambersburg PA
CBHW051817090426
42736CB00011B/1517